Peace Parity Prosperity

Peace Parity Prosperity

Avnish Kumar Bhatia

November, 2016

White Falcon Publishing
Chandigarh, India

Peace Parity Prosperity
Avnish Kumar Bhatia

White Falcon Publishing
No. 335, Sector 48-A
Chandigarh, INDIA, PIN - 160047
www.whitefalconpublishing.com

ISBN - 978-93-86210-29-6

Typeset and prepared using LaTeX 2_ε

Dedicated
To
My Mother

You were true friend to the downtrodden.

Preface

Human civilization is fraught with problems since its beginning. Crime and poverty have been the two major problems daunting human beings since time immemorial. Many other social and economic problems appear due to crime and poverty in the society. Despite all the efforts to find solutions and tremendous progress in technology, these problems persist even today.

My thinking on the ways to solve these problems started during my childhood at village Urlana Kalan, District Panipat, Haryana, India when I observed poverty and inequality in the neighbourhood. During my graduation course in agriculture at Haryana Agricultural University, Hisar from 1982 to 1986, I came in contact with communists as a member of Student Federation of India, the student wing of Communist Party of India (Marxist). They talked about equality of people under communist regimes in Russia and China. So, a communist government should be the solution to all the problems in poor countries like India. Communist ways of solving the problems advocated struggle including violence and governance with dictatorship of the exploited classes led by communist parties. Many thinkers like Mahatma Gandhi, the leader of Independence movement in India during 1918 to 1947, had advocated the progress of human society with peace and tolerance. Various religions too preach a life with truth, honesty and peaceful actions. It compelled me to think about some alternate ways of solving the problem of poverty and to bring about equality among people.

A long period after my first degree in the year 1986 passed in search of avenues for higher education and a permanent job. Finally, I joined the Indian Council of Agricultural Research as a Scientist in 1996. Subsequently, I got admission in Banaras Hindu University (BHU), Varanasi in 2000 for my Ph.D. studies in Computer Science under the supervision of Prof. S. K. Basu. The BHU campus and the Banaras City are wonderful places for education and original thinking. And I had a Ph.D. guide who was always friendly, particularly during tea time at road-side shops in the campus.

Walking in the BHU campus and along the Ghats (river banks) of Holy Ganga River was my routine. I spent time sitting at the Ghats and in the premises of New Vishwanath Temple inside the BHU campus. I kept thinking about small children working in tea shops all over India, particularly in the BHU campus and Banaras City. I wanted to understand the reason why their parents allowed the children to earn a few hundred rupees a month instead of sending them to school for primary education. The sole reason behind this sad state might be poverty. I also wanted to know the reasons why some people failed to find employment in spite of their education and skill levels, while others bagged a number of jobs to choose from.

It was here in October, 2002 when an idea struck my mind that culminated in the diagnosis and possible cure of problems of crime and poverty in the human society. The whole idea was that some people cannot adjust to the rules framed by the human society. This results in making these people either live in poverty or indulge in anti-social activities. The prime solution to the societal malice is to provide maintenance allowance to each person. This will be taking care of people like a mother so that everybody accepts the rules of the society as dictates from a mother.

I started reading books on economics, history, psychology, and other related subjects on social problems and poverty to provide shape to my ideas. Writing of this book started in 2006 in spare time after my regular duties. During the year 2013, I came across an editorial in a daily newspaper on holding a referendum on unconditional basic income in Europe after I had finished one round of the writing. Further readings on the issue refined my ideas in the second round of writing of the book.

The book contents are organized into nine chapters. The first chapter of the book introduces the problems of human civilization, mainly crime and poverty. It also defines the terms prosperity, peace and parity in a society.

Next, a brief history of human civilization is described. It describes the overall political, economic and social conditions that have existed in different parts of the world over different ages.

Evolution of various occupations are explained in a full chapter that takes stock of occupations from the start of civilization to modern industrialized and technology-savvy society. It shows how all the occupations have evolved due to demand for a product or service in the society. Various occupations are equally important for existence of human civilization.

Categorization of human beings on the basis of rationality and organizational capability are defined and characterised in one chapter. It describes how people belonging to various categories play a role in terms of prevalence of poverty and crime in the society.

One chapter makes arguments for existence of full employment at all times in human history. It dwells on important theories of employment and their critical analysis. It attempts to explore reasons for persistence of unemployment in the society.

A chapter on existing solutions of the problems of crime and poverty narrates efforts of human beings in solving these problems over the course of history. It critically analyses the existing solutions as well.

The possible solution to the problems in the form of Universal Maintenance Allowance is suggested in a full chapter. Calculation of payment of the allowance to all members of the society in a few countries is provided to demonstrate its feasibility.

The next chapter lists and describes possible impacts of the arrangement of Universal Maintenance Allowance on poverty, crime, health, peace, international relations, environment, etc.

The last chapter presents summary of the book.

Each of the chapters is made self-contained, which has resulted in repetition of some statements. Reader of the book can go from the first chapter to the last one in one go. Alternately, chapters can be read separately.

The text has been made gender-neutral by using 'it' for a person.

Theoretical ramifications in the book are shallow and data analysis is crude, which can be refined further. Nevertheless, crude realities are better than refined imaginations.

The examples and instances given in the book may relate to the Indian society. However, all the human societies have similar politico-economic problems and rules. So, descriptions in the book should apply to the entire humanity.

The book presents the facts seen and felt around us as members of the human society. Utmost care has been taken not to hurt feelings of any human-being while describing thoughts on various problems and the solution in the form of universal maintenance allowance. Still, I regret any statement that might hurt sentiments of any person on the globe.

The text may be taken in right spirit for solving the problems of human civilization for the present as well as for all the future times.

Acknowledgement

I am indebted to my mother who inculcated in me rational thinking and consideration for humanity. She always listened to the downtrodden and suggested them a path to come out of their problems.

I am thankful to my communist friends as a member of Students Federation of India at Haryana Agricultural University, Hisar during July, 1982 to June, 1986. In their company I received education on Communist and Marxist ideas along with my studies for graduate course in agricultural sciences.

My interactions with Dr. Bhikari Chand Panda at Indian Agricultural Research Institute, New Delhi during 1994-95 are duly acknowledged. His supportive attitude always encouraged individuals to talk openly and perform their best.

I am indebted to the land of Varanasi in general and Banaras Hindu University in particular, which is the land of education and knowledge. I express my gratitude to Professor Swapan Kumar Basu, my Ph.D. supervisor who tolerated my off-the-track views during December, 2000 to November, 2003 at Banaras Hindu University, Varanasi, which had the hidden ideas revealed in the book. I am also thankful to my friends during my stay at Varanasi.

I am grateful to Dr. Birham Prakash and Dr. Dinesh Kumar Yadav to have discussions at tea time at ICAR - National Bureau of Animal Genetic Resources, Karnal where I am employed as a scientist since October, 1996.

I am thankful to my neighbours Mr. Gurcharan Singh, Mr.

Balbir Singh Lather and Mr. Karan Singh for discussions during evening walk in Atal Park in Karnal.

I thank my wife Neelam, daughter Vandana and son Atal for their support and faith in me.

The help from the publisher in bringing out this book is thankfully acknowledged.

Avnish Kumar Bhatia

Contents

Chapter-1: Problems of Civilized Society

1.1 Introduction

Charles Darwin presented theory of natural evolution in his book *On the Origin of Species* published in 1859 AD. The theory states the process of evolution of various organisms from unicellular life to plants and large animals. All organisms reproduce a number of off-springs, each with a different set of characteristics, which are a result of genetic processes of mutation and recombination. Some newly-born individuals are equipped with characteristics that make them strong enough to adapt to the surrounding environment consisting of climate, food, territory, etc. Strong individuals in terms of adaptation to the environment survive and grow to reproduce children while weaker individuals die out without further reproduction. Thus, strong parents pass on their characteristics to their off-springs. Over a number of generations, small physical changes resulting from mutation and crossover spread throughout the population. The evolution process causes growth of fitter population in a species as well as formation of new species over time. Species that cannot adapt to changes in environmental conditions vanish from the earth.

Humans have also evolved as wild creatures over the course of natural evolution some time around six million years ago. Modern humans began to appear about one million years ago after migration from Africa to various regions of Asia and

Europe. Human beings made advances in living, which resulted in formation of civilized society over thousands of years. New types of tools made of stones and bones appeared about forty thousand years ago. Creation of art and elaborate rituals also started at the same time. The period around 10000 B.C. was the start of Neolithic (New Stone) Age, which was characterized by domestication of animals, introduction of agriculture, weaving, stone polishing, pottery making, and construction of permanent habitation.

Human civilization has passed through various phases from primitive hunters and gatherers to modern sophisticated society. It has experienced phases of agricultural society and industrialized society to the modern age of Internet, mobile communication, sophisticated weaponry including laser-guided equipments, atom bomb, and space travel. Various requirements of humans have evolved to the present state through the course of civilization. Techniques for requirement of food, agriculture, clothing, education, transportation, communication, law, justice, entertainment, sports, banking, business, etc. have evolved in stages to the present state and are still evolving towards perfection.

Despite all these advancements in technology, some problems of human society haunt human civilization. These problems can be listed as poverty, crime, health, injustice, wars, etc. A number of social problems of the American society are described in Eitzen & Zinn (1997), which include population growth, environmental degradation, poverty, racial inequality, gender inequality, sexual orientation, unemployment, education, health, national security, drugs, crime and justice. Some new problems such as terrorism, climate change have appeared during recent times.

Poverty and crime are the two most serious problems that have persisted during the course of civilized society. All the other problems are manifestation of poverty and crime.

Both poverty and crime are as old as the human civilization. There are numerous statements on the two problems in history.

Hellenistic world of Alexander the great and after had a large class of poor people. Rome at the height of Roman Empire during 27 BC had a large proportion of poor population who lived in multi-story wooden apartments. Many slaves and agricultural workers led miserable lives in Roman society. There were homeless people at the heyday of Chinese civilization during 12th century AD Sung dynasty who begged for food. The government had to open hospitals and orphanages for the poor. Poverty was a serious problem in Chinese cities during floods or famines when peasants migrated to cities.

Poverty existed during the Industrial revolution in eighteenth century AD. Working and living conditions of labourers were pathetic during the course of the Industrial revolution. Poverty is prevalent in modern society also. There are stories of poverty and hunger in daily tabloids all over the world.

At the same time, societies have attempted to contain these problems. All the religion of the world have described pathetic conditions of poverty and called upon followers to be kind to the poor. During medieval age of feudalism from eighth to fifteenth century AD, the church took charge of helping the poor people. Monasteries gave gifts of food and clothing to the poor.

Hammurabi, the ruler of Babylon during 1800 BC passed a collection of law to contain crime. The Jewish code of Ten Commandments developed around 1500 BC included the point of being kind to the poor. The Sanskrit texts of *Dharmaśāstra* during 1250 BC are an elaborate source of legal code where issues such as legal and religious duties, code of conduct, penalties and remedies, etc. have been discussed. Romans had developed a code of twelve tables to control crime in the society, which were modified and extended to fit customs of people throughout the provinces under the Roman empire.

1.1.1 Poverty

Poverty has been the most serious problem of the human society. Poverty in the life of a human is a situation when it cannot fulfil daily subsistence requirements of food, clothing and housing in a civilized society. The problem has existed since ages of primitive human societies.

The problem of poverty exists even today in various forms in all the countries of the world.   In underdeveloped as well as in developing countries, a large proportion of the population do not possess enough earnings to eat a full meal during the day. Their children die due to want of food, malnutrition and health facilities. A good proportion of population can feed themselves but lack resources to arrange nutritious food, sufficient clothing and all-weather housing.   They also fail to arrange education, health, electricity, transport and other facilities. Table 1.1 shows the proportion of population living below national poverty line in some developing countries. About 21.4% of the population lived below the national poverty line in Brazil in the year 2009 while in Mexico the proportion of poverty was as high as 51.3% in 2010.

At the same time, a good proportion of population remains hungry or undernourished in developing countries, as shown in the table 1.2. There were 25 million hungry people comprising of 17 percent of the population in Bangladesh during 2010-12.

Poverty results in occurrence of numerous other problems in the society. Poor people have less money to spend on essential nutritious food. Poverty causes a third of population go hungry in many underdeveloped and developing countries. It causes health problems in poor people who consume inadequate diet.   They exhibit high infant mortality rates. Food supplies are adequate in almost all the countries of the world. In fact, there is no shortage of food when there is internal as well as external peace in a country. But poor people do not have resources to buy enough food to maintain their daily requirement.

Table 1.1: Percentage of the population living below the national poverty line in developing countries. Source: World Bank Databank.

Country	Year	Population (%)
Brazil	2009	21.4
Cambodia	2007	30.1
Colombia	2011	34.1
India	2010	29.8
Mexico	2010	51.3
Peru	2011	27.8
Sudan	2009	46.5
Vietnam	2010	20.7

Chronic hunger and malnutrition results in shorter life expectation and lower mental capabilities. Children in poor families face protein, vitamin and mineral deficiencies in their early years when brain develops to its maximum size. Vitamin deficiencies make them vulnerable to a number of diseases. They remain mentally and physically weak, and cannot learn skills to take up remunerative occupations.

The poor cannot spend money on education, and remain illiterate and unskilled. It prevents them from being employed in highly remunerative occupations.

Poor people face the problem of housing also. Most of them remain without a proper all-weather house. They create houses out of thatch, paper, and bamboo on public land and on road side land. This results in mushrooming of slum settlements commonly visible in cities and metropolitan areas in a number of poor countries. There are no public facilities like water, sanitation,

Table 1.2: Hungry\undernourished population in developing countries during the period 2010-12. Source: Food and Agriculture Organization Hunger Portal - (http://www.fao.org/hunger).

Country	Undernourished Population	
	(in million)	(% of population)
Bangladesh	25	17
China	158	12
Haiti	5	45
Pakistan	35	20
Peru	3	11
Uzbekistan	2	6
Zimbabwe	4	33
World	868	13

toilets, etc. in these slums. This creates many more problems of sanitation that lead to outbreak of epidemics. Their sufferings become worst during adverse weather conditions of winter and rainy season.

Poverty also causes loss of peace in societies. Poor people lose trust in the government. They agitate for employment and facilities, disturbing peace in the society.

The form of poverty is different in industrialized and developed societies of Europe, America and Japan. Poor people in these countries have sufficient to eat and cloth themselves, but may not possess enough housing and health facilities. In United States of America, one is poor if it lives with a standard of living below the minimum income required for maintenance of adequate diet, health and shelter. Poverty in High Income Countries is typically measured in relative terms, and not in absolute terms. National poverty lines are generally defined in terms of percentage points of median income.

There are around 170 million people living in poverty as

locally defined in High Income Countries, which makes 11 per cent of global poverty. Table 1.3 displays the proportion of population living below official national poverty line in some developed countries. Australia had 4.58 million people living below the national poverty line in the year 2007, which made 21.7 percent of population in the country.

Poor people in developed countries suffer more during phases of recession when it becomes difficult to find employment. Governments provide food-aid to poor people, particularly children in these countries during recession.

Table 1.3: Population living below the national poverty line in developed countries. Source: Gentilini & Sumner (2012).

Country	Year	Population below poverty line	
		(in Million)	(% of population)
Australia	2007	4.58	21.70
Belgium	2010	1.57	14.60
France	2010	8.21	13.50
Greece	2010	2.21	20.10
United Kingdom	2010	10.52	17.10
United States of America	2010	46.18	15.10

Poor societies exhibit higher levels of inequality in income and wealth distribution. Income inequality is measured by Gini coefficient. It can take any value between 0 and 1. The value of Gini coefficient equal to zero indicates complete equality while the value equal to one indicates complete inequality. Table 1.4 shows values of Gini coefficients for personal income in some countries. The measure of Gini coefficient is equal to 0.70 for South Africa while the value is 0.27 for Belgium. A higher level of inequality indicates prevalence of extreme poverty in the society.

Table 1.4: Gini coefficient for personal income in various countries. Source: United Nations (2012); OECD (2011).

Country	Year	Gini coefficient
Australia	late-2000s	0.34
Belgium	late-2000s	0.27
France	late-2000s	0.29
United Kingdom	late-2000s	0.34
United States of America	late-2000s	0.37
South Africa	2005	0.70
India	2010	0.48
Bangladesh	2005	0.40
China	2009	0.47

1.1.2 Crime

Crime is another problem of the human civilization that gives birth to numerous other problems. Crime is any action by human beings, which is in deviation of rules of contemporary civilized society. An action may be perceived as crime in a society at a time period while it may be an accepted activity in another society or at a different time period in the same society. Working against human rights is a crime in modern society while it was not a crime in ancient society. Slavery and inhuman treatment of war prisoners have been accepted in many societies as late as seventeenth century AD.

Crime destroys stability in civilized society because it makes people lose faith in rules of the society. It becomes difficult to maintain order in the society due to acts of crime. Thieves and robbers loot the hard earned belongings of others. Thus, it creates disbelief for hard work in the society. Similarly, white-collar crimes like bribery and tax-evasion make people lose faith in political and economic system in the civilized society. Drug-trafficking makes persons drug-addicts and aggravates situation of disorder in the society as these addicts indulge in crimes for want of money to purchase drugs. They do not believe in value of labour. Crimes cause physical and sexual assaults such as injury, rape and even murder. Such heinous crimes disturb order of the society. It causes physical injuries and psychological illness among victims and they lose faith in civilized social system. Institutions of marriage and family get disturbed due to sexual crimes, thus destroying the whole social order.

In extreme cases, organized criminals create a parallel political and economic system in the society. General members of the society have to bear it due to power of such gangs. This situation creates psychological weakness in the whole society, affecting overall production, income and well-being of the society. Some gangs of people organize terrorism in the society and disturb peace and social order. Terrorism has compelled populations to migrate from their native places to face hardships and poverty on other lands.

Table 1.5 displays rates of various crimes in some countries. Even the developed countries of the world are not crime free. United States of America recorded 5.9 murders per 100,000 people in the year 2004. New Zealand reported a rate of 0.315 rapes per 1000 people in 2008.

Table 1.5: Crime rates in various countries. Source: http://www.nationmaster.com/index.php.

Crime	Country	Year	Incidence
Murders	South Africa	2004	69.0
(per 100,000)	Brazil	2004	30.8
	Sri Lanka	2004	7.2
	United States of America	2004	5.9

	United Arab Emirates	2004	0.7
Rapes	New Zealand	2008	0.315
(per 1000)	Ireland	2008	0.102
	Russia	2008	0.050
	Japan	2008	0.014
	Egypt	2008	0.001
Frauds	United Kingdom		358,186
	Mexico		61,970
	India		41,403
	Greece		391
	Kuwait		140
Drug offences	Germany		250,969
(per 100,000)	Italy		37,965
	Argentina		15,508
	Thailand		428.9
	China		3.9

1.2 Prosperity

A society can be called without extreme poverty when each of its members can afford enough food, clothing and all-weather housing. Many of the industrialized societies of America and Europe are out of extreme poverty. Countries in other parts of the world in Asia, Africa still populate extremely poor people.

A society can be called prosperous when each of its members possesses enough resources to purchase all the permitted goods and services, which are produced using contemporary skills and technology, and are available in the market.

It is not possible for a member of the society to purchase each of the goods and services available in the market. But in a prosperous society, each person should possess enough resources so as to enable him to purchase each available item. It is then up to the people to make decisions on what to purchase and what not to purchase as a consumer. Economic laws of marginal utility and substitution effect of goods help him in making these decisions.

A rational person will consume the basket of goods and services that provides maximum satisfaction with expenditure of an additional unit of money. There are a number of choices of goods and services in the market to satisfy the same requirement. Some of the goods and services can be substituted with each other. A rational person will select those goods and services to satisfy its needs so as to draw maximum satisfaction out of available resources.

In the situation of prosperity, a person should be able to purchase any type of food item, clothing, housing, jewellery, air-travel, passenger car, health facilities, education, etc. for self and its children. But it is not possible to purchase everything available in the market. Now, it is for an individual to make a decision what to purchase at this moment of time so as to draw maximum satisfaction from the consumption of goods and services with the quantum of money in the pocket.

There is no country today that fulfils the above definition of prosperity. A good proportion of population in developed countries is below national poverty line, which does not possess enough money to purchase each of the goods and services available in the market. Some of the poor people cannot purchase required housing. Others cannot afford costly health facilities.

1.3 Peace

A situation of peace indicates that there is mutual trust among members of the society. Everybody does its job honestly to the best of one's abilities. Each individual believes in truthfulness and loyalty of others. So, there is no quarrel among members of the society. Differences, if any, are sorted out with mutual dialogue.

All members of the society recognise and respect earnings and belongings of the others. There are no cases of theft or burglary in the society.

In a peaceful society, all the members should abide by rules of the society. The person violating any rule intentionally or inadvertently is ready to admit the mistake in front of the law enforcing authorities as well as in a court of justice. Everybody is willing to accept the punishment announced on him after trial in a court.

No society on the globe has reached this definition of peace. There are high crime rates even in rich countries while some of the poor countries have lower crime rates. All the countries have to maintain policing round the clock. A number of security gadgets such as camera, alarm, lock, etc. are used to keep a watch on offenders of law. Courts are overwhelmed by cases of crimes and conflicts.

1.4 Parity

The condition of parity in a society is consequent to the conditions of peace and prosperity. In a prosperous society with peaceful life, all the human beings should be equal in terms of the ability to purchase each item of consumption as well as the ability to live a life without quarrel and fear.

A few members of the society may be far richer in terms of income and wealth compared to many other members of the society. But all the individuals in a prosperous society can afford to purchase all the goods and services available in the market. Therefore, level of enjoyment and happiness would be equal among all the members of the society. Disparity would be exhibited only as people in possession of more resources having an edge over others in terms of commanding higher status and respect in the society.

At the same time, all the human beings respect and follow the laws of society. The government, police and judicial systems can manage conflicts to the satisfaction of everybody. Each member is practically equal in getting justice in the society. So, peace prevails in the society.

Thus, prosperity along with peace would ensure parity of all the human beings in a civilized society.

Human civilization aims to diagnose and treat the problems of poverty and crime. Civilized society without these problems should lead to the conditions of peace, parity and prosperity.

Chapter-2: A Brief History of Civilization

2.1 Beginning of Civilization

There are a number of theories on the origin of humans. Some of the theories estimate the origin of human beings a few thousand years ago. Others state it as millions of years old event. Darwin's theory of natural evolution is the most accepted and scientific one, which states that man has evolved like other organisms through the processes of natural selection aided by mutation in genotypes. Thus, human-beings have evolved to the present form through the processes of natural evolution like other species of higher animals be it horse, elephant, dog, monkey, etc.

Humans wandered like other animals in search of food in the form of fruits, seeds and nuts. Later, hunting of animals and fishing also became sources of food. They indulged in sex and reproduction of children like other animals such as dog, lion, cat, elephant, etc. They wandered without any clothes and had food and sex without any civil rules, meaning there was no form of civilization to name.

Slowly, human-beings started living in natural caves to save themselves from deadly animals and vagaries of weather. They started making tools from wood, animal bones and stones around forty thousand years ago that helped in hunting of animals. They started wearing clothes made of skin obtained from plants and animals. Knowledge about use of fire made man more secure and taste-loving creature. They developed the habit of storing food for a few days. It provided leisure time to draw and paint on stone walls of caves. Humans started taming and domesticating food-providing animals like goat, cattle, sheep and pig. Subsequently, they started raising crops for food-grains, pulses and fruits. Agriculture and animal husbandry were being practised during pre-historic times about 6000 years ago.

With development of agricultural practices and settled living styles, man inculcated a sense of possessiveness. It did not want to share the food collected and raised through hard work. Likewise, it started recognising sexual mate. So, it did not like the mate to have sex with others. In this way, the institution of marriage started to take shape. Once married, the couple started recognising their children. This led to development of the institution of family.

By this time, humans were using various tools for animal hunting, livestock rearing and raising crops. It had also developed some weapons such as bow and arrow for hunting and fighting. It started using metals to make weapons and utensils. Groups were formed to gain control of land, water, hunting grounds and other natural resources. Thus, many people started living together in communities. They developed rules to regulate their lives, which included the rules to grow, store and consume food. Rules were also framed for indulging in sex, contracting marriage and family life.

Irrigation systems were developed to ensure food supply amid vagaries of weather. With improvement in farming and animal husbandry, workers developed skills in the society to make tools. Some of the people started moving agricultural produce, tools and implements from one place to the other for exchange with goods produced elsewhere, which led to emergence of trade.

Despite the advancements in civilization, humans continued to face uncertainties in life. Firstly, uncertainties in nature in the form of natural calamities disturbed time and again. Secondly, attacks from other communities destroyed the hard earned and stored food along with other belongings. The third problem was miscreants within the community who disobeyed the rules of society regarding food and sex. A few other problems such as diseases and health issues were worrisome in the newly-found luxurious life.

People learned to work together to fight natural calamities like flood and drought in a cooperative manner. Cooperation was also required to fight external attacks. The need for cooperation and collective actions resulted in emergence of leaders within communities who could organize collective work. The leaders organised army to fight attacks from other communities. These leaders transformed into kings over time who led a system of government in their kingdoms. The kings collected taxes, organized armies and managed collective works in the society. They also managed trade, law enforcement and diseases in their jurisdiction.

Kings framed rules of a civilized society for members of their kingdom to follow. These rules included rules of sex, family life, trade, farming, taxes, etc. Those who did not follow the rules were liable for punishment. Police and jails were created by the kings to implement the rules. Offenders of rules were brought to kings and judges appointed for the purpose of enforcing rules. Those found guilty were punished for violating rules of the society and put into jails on the basis of the nature of offences.

With all the systems of a civilized society in place, human beings could not control problems of natural calamities, health, miscreants and disobedient persons in the society. This failure of civilization by sheer force of law resulted in emergence of religion. Some people emerged as religious leaders who could explain the role of super-natural powers and gods. They narrated the effects of religious forces on human lives before and after death. With the emergence of religious ceremonies, institutions of marriage and family were established with social and religious stamps. Life situations beyond control of human beings were left to the mercy of gods. Religion also explained natural punishment to the people who did not follow the rules of the civilized society.

2.2 Emergence of City-States

The emergence of civilization was a gradual process. Early human settlements were established in small groups of tribes. Slowly, people started living in village settlements where various groups of individuals were involved in producing particular kind of products and services.

Concentrated populations in villages were able to produce surplus food, which was exported for exchange of raw material and precious items not available locally. Ambitious individuals succeeded in diverting resources into construction of monumental and ceremonial centres that provided focus for the population living near them. This caused the first appearance of cities.

City centres could develop only when people refined their ability to produce surplus food through advanced techniques of agriculture and irrigation. Therefore, the civilization first prospered in river valleys. The first civilization developed in Mesopotamia along Tigris and Euphrates rivers in South-west Asia by 4000 BC. The city centres developed in Mesopotamia in 3500 BC, in Egypt in 3100 BC, in Indus-valley in 2500 BC and in China in 1800 BC. Trade and exchange of goods were important in the expansion of city-states. Religious, political and military powers were concentrated in the hands of a few ruling families in all these civilizations.

Cities were the basic political units of power. City-states was a form of government with a town and surrounding villages it controlled. Religion became fundamental to the social organization. The cities-states established diplomatic and trade relationships with each other. Trade and gift-exchange between cities encouraged development of a common culture from the Persian Gulf to far away areas in north-west and north of the region.

Development of some form of writing occurred almost at the start of each of the civilizations. Early writings were inscribed on clay tablets. Clay inscriptions spread to Crete and Greece by around 1500 BC. Egyptians worked out a system of writing by about 3000 BC using pictures or symbols to indicate words or sounds. They also invented sheets for writing from a tree called papyrus, from which the word 'paper' has appeared.

2.3 Emergence of Empires

Towards the end of the third millennium BC, powerful leaders attempted to expand their influence over a wider area. The first of these leaders was Sargon during 2296-2240 BC, who created a new political centre at Agade before conquering the cities of southern Mesopotamia.

Hammurabi of Babylon established an empire during early part of 17th century BC. He is famous for his law code that was inscribed throughout the empire on a large stone with a carving of the king in the presence of Shamash, the Babylonian Sun-god.

Assyrian, Babylonian and Egyptian empires existed in 7th century BC when Persian state emerged in the areas of modern Iran. Persian ruler Cyrus (559-530 BC) defeated many kingdoms and gained control of the areas from Afghanistan to Greece.

Greece was transforming during 8th century BC with monumental public buildings and reintroduction of literacy. Groups of Greeks started settlements around the Mediterranean in Italy, Sicily and North Africa. Increasing wealth due to trading activities led to the emergence of powerful individuals known as tyrants in many Greek city-states. These city-states published law codes on large stone tablets. Phillip, the king of Macedonia defeated Athens and Thebes, imposing his rule in whole of Greece. After his death in 336 BC, his son Alexander united Greece from where he launched his invasion of the Persian Empire.

Alexander was an ambitious and brilliant general. By the time of his death in 323 BC at the age of 32, he was recognized as the legitimate ruler of an empire stretching from Egypt to India. By 276 BC, the empire divided into three main kingdoms - Antigonid Macedon, Seleucid Asia and Ptolemaic Egypt. India was divided among tribal republics called *Mahajanpadas* by about 500 BC. After a century of wars, the kingdom of Magadha dominated with its splendid capital of Pataliputra to be the nucleus of the first Indian empire. After Alexander's invasion in 327 BC, Mauryan prince Chandragupta seized the Magadhan throne. The Mauryan Empire reached its zenith under Ashoka, the Great who established his rule over most of the subcontinent.

Shang rulers in China arose during 1500 BC and are said to have conquered a number of city-states. China started using iron tools and animal power for cultivation from about 500 BC. This led to increased agricultural productivity, population growth, commerce and flourishing industries. Large cities emerged due to increased economic activities. Chin dynasty emerged from this period to unify China with a centralized bureaucracy to improve the production and distribution of grains, organization of construction work and an army with a ruthless penal code. The Chin king Shih Huang-ti was crowned the first emperor of China in 221 BC. His dynasty collapsed in a nationwide rebellion in 206 BC shortly after his death. A new Han dynasty copied the general principles of Chin system, but softened harshness. The 'legalist' system of rewards and punishment was replaced by Confucianism, which emphasized benevolent rule and good statesmanship.

The city of Rome established on the Tiber River started showing signs of urbanization from 7th century BC. Rome was ruled by a line of seven kings. The last king was expelled in 511 BC. This resulted in creation of a Republic ruled by two annually elected consuls who held office for a single year and ruled with the support of the Senate, a council of former consuls and priests. An assembly was there to ratify legislation and to protect the city with military campaigns. Success in wars brought gains to the people of Rome and prestige to the commanders. By 264 BC, Rome controlled the entire Italian peninsula. Romans developed naval fighting skills to defeat Carthage power in North Africa in the First Punic War during 264-241 BC. By 133 BC, Roman commanders expanded the empire from Spain in the west to Macedonia along with part of Asia in the east. The later generations of the Republic saw the system to collapse in a series of civil wars, which ended in 31 BC when Octavian, adopted son of Julius Caesar, emerged triumphant and undisputed master of Rome. In 19 BC, Octavian rechristened as Emperor Augustus was given the power to rule by decree, although he continued to pay due respect to the Senate. Assassination of Emperor Domitian was followed by nearly a century of stability. At its height in 180 AD, the Roman Empire stretched from Britannia to Egypt.

Ruling of the vast empire became so difficult that Emperor Diocletian divided it into sections ruled by co-emperors. The administrative arrangement was completed under Constantine (312-337 AD). The Western empire was administered from Rome with Latin as its language. The Eastern empire was administered from Constantinople with Greek as its language. The Western empire lost control to tribes of Germanic people. In 476 AD, the German warrior Odoacer deposed the Roman emperor, ending the Western Roman Empire. The Eastern Empire survived until the fall of Constantinople to the Turks in 1453.

Mongol tribes had lived for centuries in Asian region of Mongolia. Genghis Khan was borne around 1167 AD as the son of a minor Mongol tribe chief. He became leader of the united Turco-Mongol tribes. With light cavalry, he conducted raids from the steppe into the towns. He invaded northern China in 1211 AD, subduing Chin Empire and crossing the Great Wall. After the win, Genghis Khan unleashed bloody raids from Central Asia through Iran to the Caucasus and into the plains of Russia.

Genghis Khan divided his empire among his four sons before

his death in 1227. His grandson Batu directed the invasion of Europe. Kiev was defeated in 1240. Poland and Hungary were attacked. Mongol troops reached the coastline of Croatia when the death of Great Khan Ogodei in December, 1241 made Batu withdraw to take part in affairs of state and to participate in Grand Council.

The Mongol empire was the greatest land empire in the history. It stretched from Korea in the east to Poland in the west, from the Arctic in the North to Turkey and Persia in the south. In Persia and China, the Mongol dynasties lasted under a century, while in Russia the Golden Horde they lasted for more than 200 years.

2.4 Spread of Religions

People of the Old Stone Age during 40 to 70 thousand years ago buried their dead with tools, weapons and food, indicating that they had some kind of religion. As the institution of family developed with start of agriculture in New Stone Age 10000 years ago, religion became important part of routine activities. People believed in many gods and in the unseen forces in nature. They begged their gods to provide water and to make seeds grow.

Egyptian kings in about 3100 BC were regarded as gods and they took the title Pharaoh. Egyptians worshipped the sun and the moon. Sumerians believed in many gods. Their temples were also used as schools for education. Persians were also polytheists. About 600 BC, a great religious reformer Zoroaster completely changed their religious ideas. He taught that the world was a place where human beings were trained for a future life. There was a great struggle between the forces of good and evil. The thinking of Hebrews seems to have been affected by Zoroastrian idea of the struggle between good and evil and a final judgement in which reward or punishment depended on human choice.

The early Hebrews before 1500 BC worshipped Yahweh as a god who might be called a tribal war god. If people sinned against god, they along with their children would be punished. Later, Jews started to think of Yahweh as a loving father and a god of all people.

In the Indus-valley civilization around 2000 BC, people seem to have worshipped animals such as bulls, elephants, tigers associated with physical power and fertility. The earliest gods mentioned in the Aryan books of Vedas during 1500-1000 BC were forces of nature, such as sky, sun, earth, light, fire, wind, storm and rain. These natural forces were personified for worship. Although Vedic religion is full of references to many gods, it suggests a more sophisticated concept of god as the creator of order out of chaos in the universe. Interpretations of rituals and hymns of the Vedas were left to groups of priests called Brahman. This practice led to development of Hinduism. The major belief of Hinduism is provided by reincarnation or the transmission of souls after death. Thus, the soul lives second, third and more lives. The sufferings can be overcome by practising moral duty. Finally, good persons are rewarded, evil ones are punished.

Chinese people believed in a dragon that lived in seas and rivers at the time of Shang dynasty during 1500 to 1100 BC. The dragon was considered all powerful and kind. The Chinese were concerned with ethical issues of proper behaviour in life. They believed that their rulers received power through communication with spirits and order from them was mandate of the Heaven.

The Greeks around 1000 BC wanted to know mysteries of the physical world as thunder, lightning, change of seasons, etc. They were also interested to know about passions that caused people lose self-control and ways to gain long life, good fortune and abundant harvests. Greek gods lived on the top of mount Olympus in northern Greece. They believed that there were many gods and goddesses of equal status. At certain sanctuaries called Oracles, the gods were believed to speak through priests usually to answer questions about the future.

The religion of early Romans during 1000 BC was a form

of animism. The spirits had to be made friendly by rituals and sacrifices. The old family religion became state religion with temples, priests, and ceremonies. High priest was elected by the Assembly of Tribes. Gautam Buddha was a great religious leader born about 563 BC as an Indian prince. At the age of 29 while roaming in the city streets, he was disturbed to see an old man, a very sick man and corpse to be cremated. He wondered about sufferings of life and value of life and death. He left his palace, wife and young child to set out in search for the truth. After six years of physical discipline, self-torture and fasting, he felt that he had understood the truth while meditating under a fig tree. In that moment he became Buddha, the enlightened one.

Buddha said that salvation comes from understanding the four noble truths that are (i) suffering (ii) caused by greed and desire (iii) which can be avoided by renouncing desire to attain nirvana, the perfect peace (iv) gained by following the Middle path. The Middle path may be pursued by following eight guides, which are right views, right intentions, right speech, right action, right living, right effort, right mindfulness, and right concentration.

Buddha gained some followers in his life time. Over centuries, Buddhism won wide acceptance after the Great Ashoka, the Mauryian emperor became a devout Buddhist in about 250 BC. Ashoka's campaign to conquer all of India killed hundreds of thousands people. The emperor became sickened by this slaughter and embraced Buddhism. He sent his brother and other missionaries to Ceylon, Tibet, China, Burma, Java, Egypt, Syria and Macedonia to preach Buddhism.

Buddhism appealed to the wealthy and educated Chinese. They were attracted by its elaborate ceremonies, art and literature. Buddhism reached its highest point in China around 700 AD. Monasteries had been built with gifts of tax free land from wealthy believers. Buddhist monks introduced the religion in Japan in around 550 AD. At first, the new religion was opposed. Soon an epidemic broke out, which was taken as a sign of power of the new religion. Buddhism won many converts among nobles. Many new Buddhist sects were established, which taught that salvation was possible through faith alone. It appealed to ordinary people as well.

Jesus was born in the town of Bethlehem near Jerusalem in southern Palestine. He had been a student of the writings of Jewish prophets. He travelled through villages with a small group of disciples to preach as a wandering rabbi. He created excitement among people with miracles of healing and defending the poor and oppressed. He summarized the Hebrew Ten Commandments into two great commandments. (i) People must love god above everything else. (ii) They must love others as they love themselves.

Jesus claimed that he was the son of god. When he travelled to Jerusalem in about 30 AD, many Jews hailed him as the Messiah. Conservative Jewish priests regarded him as revolutionary. Roman governor ordered his execution by crucifixion. According to Gospels, Jesus arose from the dead and remained on earth for 40 more days before ascending to the Heaven.

Jesus disciples set out preaching his teachings through the message - Christ, the son of god had died for the sins of the human race. A Jew named Saul from Asia Minor was converted to Christianity. He took the name Paul and became a great Christian missionary. His work among Jews and other people spread the religion rapidly. Paul visited Rome where he was put to death by the emperor Nero.

Christianity was open to everyone and charged nothing. Christians were expected to be good citizens and were encouraged to practice charity and care for the poor and the outcast.

By 300 AD, the Church had grown into a well-organized body owning buildings and burial grounds. In the year 312 AD, the Roman emperor Constantine gained victory in a civil war, which he attributed to the power of Christian God. Subsequently, the Churches received many favours from the emperor, and

Christianity began to establish itself as the dominant religion of the empire.

In the fifth century, there were still many pagans who did not believe in the major religion, but Christianity spread to Roman empire through the program of church building. Meanwhile, the religion had also spread to the east to Persia and to the west among the barbarian tribes which invaded and destroyed Western Roman Empire. Franks, who were pagans, accepted Christianity around 500 AD. Orthodox Church in Byzantium in eastern Roman Empire converted Slavs of central Europe to Christianity at the end of ninth century.

In ancient times, the Arabian Peninsula was largely inhabited by nomadic tribes. They wandered in search of grazing land and water for their camels and sheep. Arabia had a number of ancient holy places where tribesmen could meet together in the sacred enclave to arrange treaties and trading. The most important of these was Kaaba, the shrine at Mecca, whose guardians were the Quraysh tribe. Prophet Muhammad, the founder of Islam was born in this tribe in 570 AD.

Muhammad received his first revelations in about 610 AD and his followers soon grew in number. However, hostility of merchants and rulers of Mecca made him and his followers to flee to Medina in 622 AD. The event is known as *hegira*. In 630 AD, he returned to Mecca in triumph. By 632 AD, when Muhammad died, almost all the Arabian tribes had accepted Islam.

The central belief of Islam is - there is no God but Allah, and Muhammad is his prophet. Koran is the holy book of Islam, which is a presentation of Muhammad's most important teachings.

Muhammad's successor, Caliph Abu Bakr completed the conquest of Arabia and advanced to Palestine. Caliph Omar advanced to Damascus, which was followed by victory over Byzantine. By 643 AD, Persia had been overrun. The conquest of Herat and fall of Kabul opened the way to Sind in India in 712 AD. Simultaneously, Arab forces pushed west into Egypt and advancing through North Africa crossed the strait of Gibraltar in 711 AD and conquered the southern part of Spain. Raids into southern France were deflected by Franks. Initially, Islam did not insist upon conversion. Under the Abbasid dynasty during 750-1258 AD, however large scale conversions to Islam became common. About the year 1000 AD Turkish Muslim rulers of Afghanistan began invading India through the north-west mountain passes. Muslims used riders on horseback and occupied Delhi in 1193, and by 1236 they controlled all of the northern India.

2.5 Colonialism

During seventeenth and eighteenth centuries, European rulers became dominating and conquered ancient empires around the world. European colonists and traders were influential on every continent. The expansion of European civilization transformed relations among people, which was one of the most significant developments in history.

Europeans traded with Arabs during middle ages in order to buy valuable spices and silk, and with Asians to buy jewels. By late 15th century, they developed the ability to explore foreign lands. Their goal was to get to India and adjoining regions in Asia in order to acquire valuable trading items such as spices, silk and jewels.

Map making had improved because of pictorial accuracy and writings of ancient geographers. Equally important were navigation instruments, which helped ships to sail far in the sea. In 1300s, a true compass was made by fixing a magnet to a card, which passed to Europe through Arabs from Chinese inventions. In 1400, European ships were inferior to those of Arabs, Indians and Chinese. But by 1600, the Europeans made the best ships in the world. By this time European rulers had the power, wealth and will to support persons sailing for explorations.

Standardization of money made economic transactions much more stable and reliable. A large sum of money was accumulated in banks. Lending by banks and availability of money made financing of huge overseas explorations possible. Increase in population in Europe also made peasants leave their villages in search of better opportunities as sailors.

Ferdinand and Isabella, the rulers of Spain, financed a voyage by Christopher Columbus, an Italian navigator. In August, 1492 Columbus set sail from Spain towards the western direction so as to reach India quickly. He crossed the Atlantic Ocean to land in October on a tiny island in the Caribbean Sea, which he named San Salvador. He believed the islands to be off the coast of India. Actually, he had discovered the island later known as West Indies.

In the early 1400s Prince Henry of Portugal founded a school for training of navigators. His sea captains began a series of explorations west-ward into the Atlantic and south-ward along the western coast of Africa. These explorations brought big gains to the Portuguese. In 1498, Vasco da Gama sailed around Africa and crossed the Indian Ocean to reach India. He came home with a fabulous cargo of spices and jewels. Portuguese captain Petro Alvares Cabral reached the east coast of South America in 1500.

Between 1497 and 1503 Amerigo Vespucci, an Italian took part in several Portuguese expeditions across the Atlantic. He became convinced that the land he saw was not part of Asia and described it as the 'New World'. Later, a German geographer named the new land 'America' after Vespucci's first name.

Newly discovered lands were waiting to be settled. European exploration was result of the desire to gain wealth and the wish to spread Christianity. However, the wish to gain wealth became more important over time.

Portuguese set up a colony in Angola. They set up trading posts on the eastern coast of Africa including Mozambique and Zanzibar. About the year 1510, they conquered south-east coast of India and began to use its port of Goa as trading and administrative centre. They conquered Malacca on the south-west coast of Malaya in south-east Asia. It gave them a base to push on to China where they landed in 1514. The contemporary Ming dynasty in China was following a policy of isolation and expelled the Portuguese several times. Finally, they were allowed to establish a trading post on an island.

Portuguese gained foothold in Ceylon, off the south-east coast of India, which was important as a stopping point between Goa and Malacca. The island was also a source of tea and spices.

In Brazil in South America, the Portuguese founded a much larger colony. The huge country was divided by them into enormous agricultural estates to grow sugar for export. Labour force on these farms consisted of slaves.

The Spaniards turned most of their energies to America. They explored West Indies, Central America and parts of the mainland of North and South America. They did not find spices there, for which they had explored the foreign lands. However, the soil was fertile and there were numerous minerals. They were able to control the native population. Unfortunately, they destroyed the native people and their remarkable civilizations.

Nations of Northern Europe started late to establish colonies due to their preoccupation with internal problems.

The King of England commissioned an Italian Captain named John Cabot for voyage to North America. In 1497-98, he explored the coasts of Newfoundland, Nova Scotia and New England in the New World. In 1600, Queen Elizabeth granted a charter to a trading company called English East India Company. The company set up trading posts at Bombay, Calcutta and Madras in India. The company dealt with local rulers cunningly. Where a ruler was weak, the company gave aid to it. Where force was needed, it was used without any hesitation. If bribery was better means to influence, a generous gift was offered.

English explorations into North America were made in search of a passage to India. In the process, the English became interested in North America and began to establish colonies there. A number of English colonies were set up along the east coast of North America during 1600s. These settlements were established for commercial purposes.

In 1602 the Dutch combined several of their companies into Dutch East India Company. The company had sole right to carry on trade between northern Netherlands and Africa and East Indies. The Dutch made settlements in the islands of Java, Sumatra and eastward to seize the valuable spice islands from the Portuguese. Subsequently, Malacca, Ceylon and Cochin on south-west coast of India were also conquered. In 1652 the Dutch also founded a colony at the southern tip of Africa.

French colonies in North America developed slowly until later half of 1600s. They explored Great Lakes region, and inland region of North America named as Louisiana. French set up sugar producing colonies in West Indies. French East India Company was formed in 1664, which established a trading post in Pondicherry on the south-east coast of India.

Russia grew in the east direction towards Central Asia. Russia's eastward expansion was carried on mostly by nomadic, freedom loving people called Cossacks. In 1581, a group of Cossacks conquered the city of Sibir on the east side of Ural Mountains. This led them to the entire region east of Ural known as Siberia. By the 1640s the Russian had reached the Pacific Ocean.

2.6 Revolutions

A number of local and short lived revolutions have occurred in the history. But the American Revolution and the French Revolution in 18th century have continued to inspire people in later generations. Russian revolution in 1917 also affected humanity for many years.

In his book 'The Social Contract' in 1762, French philosopher

Rousseau articulated that just laws and wise government must be based on the free choice of people. Another French writer Voltaire advocated religious toleration and freedom of speech. These ideas swept the world to revolutions against existing regimes.

In 1774, Britain passed a series of laws that were intolerable to colonies. One of the acts closed the port of Boston to all shipping so as to promote only British goods in America. Delegates from colonies met in Philadelphia in the first Continental Congress demanding full rights for British people living in colonies. Delegates to the Second Congress voted to declare their freedom from Great Britain. In 1775, British American colonies rebelled against the existing tax regime. On July 4, 1776, they adopted the Declaration of Independence, which established the United States of America as an independent nation.

After the Declaration of Independence, fighting between the British and the Americans became a revolutionary war. Americans fought a six year war under the leadership of George Washington against British forces, finally winning independence in 1783. Most of the war was fought between 1776-1781. Finally the British accepted many of the peace terms offered by Benjamin Franklin, the chief American negotiator. Treaty of Paris was signed in 1783 in which the Americans won much larger area than the original 13 states.

The Americans established a modern constitutional republic based on ideas of human rights and equality.

In 1789, the most powerful French monarchy in Europe was overthrown by a popular revolution. The French revolution had many long-term as well as immediate causes. For 30 years, there had been peasants hostility to rising rents in France. By the 1780s, the language of liberty had permeated to educated elites, gentry and bourgeois. Craftsmen and shopkeepers started articulating their political and economic grievances in terms of civil rights and economic justice.

French Monarchy had increased level of central control and

fiscal demand due to failure in war and poor harvests. The Monarch Louis XVI called the assembly of Estate Generals representing the clergy - the First Estate, gentry - the Second Estate, and commoners - the Third Estate. On 17 June, 1789, the Third Estate declared themselves to be the National Assembly and overturned national absolutism. On 14 July, 1789, royal prison at Bastille was stormed. In August, feudal privilege was abolished and Declaration of the Rights of Man was announced, which promised individual liberty. Louis XVI reluctantly accepted a parliamentary constitution and abolition of the structure of privilege.

During the next two years, the National Assembly formed a new constitution. The Assembly nationalized extensive land holdings of the Church. Churches were brought under state control. Nobles left France to seek aid from foreign rulers to work against the Revolution. On 20 June, 1791, King Louis and Queen Marie Antoinette made an attempt to flee out of France. Both were caught and brought back to prison. Their intention was to lead a royal army of nobles back to France to destroy the Revolution and re-establish the ancient regime. The king was executed after a trial by the National Assembly.

Russia had faced revolutionary disturbances throughout 1800s. The Revolution of 1905 had brought about apparent changes in the country. Duma, the elected legislative body was given little powers. Czar remained an absolute ruler.

In the World War I during 1914-1917, over two million Russians were killed, 5 millions were wounded and more than 2 millions were taken prisoners by the enemy. By the spring of 1917, the Russians were disheartened by appalling casualties. They had lost faith in their government and Czar Nicholas II. Strikes and street demonstrations broke out in Petrograd. Czar ordered to put them down by force. When Duma demanded reforms in government, Czar ordered its dissolution. Soldiers joined the rioters. In March, 1917, unable to control his subjects or the army,

Nicholas II was abdicated. He and his family were executed the following year, ending 300 years old Romanov dynasty in Russia. A liberal provisional government was set up to rule the country. Petrograd Soviet of Workers' and Solders' Deputies was organized when disorder began in Russia. The council was composed of moderate socialists called Mensheviks. Most of the radical socialists known as the Bolsheviks lived outside of Russia, having been exiled during the 1905 revolution. Leader of Bolsheviks was N. Lenin, who returned to Russia on April 16, 1917 from exile in Switzerland. He favoured a modified Marxism that advocated dictatorship of workers. His slogan 'Land, Peace and Bread' reached the heart of people.

In November 1917, Bolsheviks overthrew the provisional Russian government. The revolution was called Bolshevik revolution. In the spring of 1918, Bolsheviks renamed themselves as the Communist Party.

Communists faced opposition from former aristocrats, middle class liberals and Mensheviks. The communists had adopted red as their colour. Those who opposed communists were called whites. Red Army and several White armies fought many battles leaving a trail of destruction. By 1921, the communists had completely defeated the white forces.

Russian capital was moved from Petrograd to Moscow. A cabinet headed by Lenin was formed and a National Congress was established. In 1922, communist leaders gave Russia a new name, Union of Soviet Socialist Republics (USSR), as the power had to be transferred to soviets. Socialism was the guiding economic system of USSR.

2.7 Civil Rules and Laws

The earliest written civil rules pertain to Babylonian emperor Hammurabi who came to power in about 1792 BC. Hammurabi Code had 282 laws. People who failed to cultivate their fields were liable to be punished under the law. There were laws dealing with property rights, contracts and bankruptcy. Laws also dealt with marriage and divorce. Mode of punishment was harsh. If a man caused another to lose an eye, then his own eye was put out. However, wealthy people were let off merely by paying a fine.

Jewish code of laws included Ten Commandments developed around 1500 BC by the great leader Moses. Mosaic Law also demanded an eye for an eye, but it set higher value for human life. It accepted slavery and required kindness for slaves. It also required kindness for poor and strangers. Witchcraft and sacrifices to idols were crimes punishable by death.

Roman Code contained twelve tables, which were modified and expanded in two ways. New laws were passed when required, and judges interpreted the old laws to fit new circumstances. Roman law established an idea that an accused person is considered innocent unless proven guilty. Roman system of law became the foundation of laws of all European countries later. It also had a strong influence on laws of the Christian Church. The Eastern Roman Empire of Byzantine preserved the Roman law. Scholars collected and organized Roman law as the Corpus Juris Civilis (in Latin for 'Body of Civil Law'). It forms the basis of many modern European legal systems.

Edward I, the King of England during 1237-1307 AD, divided court into three branches. The Court of the Exchequer kept financial accounts and tried tax cases. The Court of Common Pleas tried private citizens cases. The Court of King's Bench heard cases that concerned the king or the government. Each of these courts handed out many verdicts. Important verdicts were collected and written down, which became the basis of future decisions in courts. This type of law was known as the Common Law because it was common to all England. It forms the basis for present day legal systems in England and many other countries.

Napoleon ruled France during 1799-1814 AD. His scholars completed revision and organization of all French laws begun by the National Convention. It abolished feudalism and serfdom in Europe. This system called The Napoleonic Code still forms the foundation of the law of many European and other countries.

2.8 Philosophy and Science

About 6000 years ago, people in the Nile valley and the Tigris-Euphrates valley made copper weapons, tools, utensils and jewellery. Bronze was used in Egypt 5000 years ago, and also at an early date in India and China. Bronze sculpture of the Indus-valley shows a fine artistic ability during 2000 BC. Indus valley people had a written language consisting of pictogram as early as about 2300 BC. People in these great river valleys developed calendars in their history. Sumerians used sun-dried clay bricks to build houses. Their buildings known as ziggurats were built on specially-constructed hills on flat lands of valley. They were the first people to use wheel. They developed algebra and a calendar with 12 months based on the movement of the moon.

Kung Fu-tse, the Chinese philosopher commonly known as Confucius, lived about 551 to 478 BC. His ideas exerted powerful influence on later Chinese life. He believed that every person should perform his assigned duties in the society. Secondly, the government should be virtuous and concerned for others. His teachings took on religious significance in the Chinese society.

Chinese astronomers computed the year equal to $365\frac{1}{4}$ days around 444 BC. In 28 BC, they observed sunspots.

The Greeks are honoured for their artistic and intellectual achievements. Socrates lived in Athens from 469-399 BC. He wanted people to learn to think. People must depend on their reasons to guide their lives. His great student Pluto wrote his ideas in the form of dialogues. In each dialogue, Socrates usually asks questions on government, education, justice, virtue and religion. Plato's student Aristotle was a great scientist and philosopher. He was skilful at definitions and in grouping related facts. He collected, described and classified plants and animals. He wrote about politics, ethics, poetics and logic.

In 500 BC, Greek philosopher and mathematician Pythagoras wrote that everything could be explained with numbers. He is best known for the Pythagorean Theorem in geometry. Greek philosopher Democritus believed that all matter is composed of moving atoms. Hippocrates is considered the founder of medicine. He taught that disease comes from natural causes and not as punishment from gods. The best cure of disease was rest, fresh air, and a proper diet.

Greek culture mixed with Mediterranean cultures during Alexander's empire during 300s BC is known as Hellenistic age. Remarkable advances were made in philosophy and science during this period. Euclid developed geometric theorems and his book 'Elements' was used for a thousand years. Archimedes used geometry to measure spheres and cones. He calculated value of *pi*, that is the relation between diameter and circumference of a circle. Hellenistic scientists added immensely to the medical knowledge. Alexandrian physicians studied nervous system and performed delicate surgery using pain killers. Aristarchus believed that the earth moves around the sun. Hipparchus of Rhodes calculated times of the eclipses of the sun and the moon. He was the first person to make systematic use of trigonometry. Hellenistic geographers told that the earth was round. Eratosthenes calculated the diameter of the earth with an error of one percent. He also claimed that people could reach India by sailing westward around the world.

Romans mainly used Greek knowledge of philosophy and science. Galen, a physician in Rome, wrote several volumes that summarized all the medical knowledge during 100s AD. A scientist from Alexandria, Ptolemy believed that the earth was at the centre of the Universe, which was an accepted theory till 1600s AD.

Gupta's rule in India during 320-535 AD has been called the

Golden age due to the brilliant civilization. Indians invented the Arabic numeral system - 1 through 9 and zero. They also had a concept of negative numbers. Aryabhata in 400s AD computed the value of *pi* more accurately than Greek mathematicians. Indian astronomers identified seven planets seen with naked eyes. They also predicted eclipses, calculated diameter of the earth and developed a theory of gravity. Indian physicians had known the importance of the spinal chord. They understood the technique of inoculation, which was unknown to Europeans until the end of 1700s. Susruta, a great Indian doctor, during this period practised strict cleanliness before an operation and used to sterilize wounds.

Arabs in the Muslim World tried to combine science and philosophy of Greece, Rome, and Asia. The great era of Muslim culture lasted from about 700-1000 AD. They learned paper making from Chinese. In 900s, Rhazes, a Muslim physician of Baghdad wrote about surgery, diseases of eyes, smallpox and measles. Muslims perfected algebra as a science. They learned Arabic numerals from mathematicians of India and transmitted it to Europe.

Arab geographical studies adapted a Hindu idea that each hemisphere of the world had a centre that was equally distant from the four cardinal points of north, south, east, and west. This theory was used by Columbus in the 1500s AD to conclude that the earth was not flat.

There was little progress in science and philosophy in Europe during Middle Ages of feudalism after decline of the Roman empire till 15th century. However, there were some important technological advances such as invention of plough, the windmill, clock and eyeglasses. It was for the Arabs to preserve the great accomplishments of Hellenistic Age.

During 1350 to 1700, started a movement on revival of interest in the classical learning of Greece and Rome, which is known as Renaissance - meaning rebirth.

The Italian scholars of the 1300s studied literature and believed that they could learn from the Greeks and Romans about human virtue and moral conduct. They searched out Greek and Roman manuscripts that had been neglected for centuries. They thought that ancient people can be imitated to be virtuous like them. These readings and thoughts brought new enthusiasm in life. They thought that men and women were intelligent beings who could make their own decisions. These studies were called humanities and those who pursued them were called humanists.

New ideas were passed along by means of new invention of printing. Started in China hundreds of years before, Arabs learned the technique and passed on to Europe where printing began to appear in 15th century.

In 1556, the English humanist Thomas More published a book - Utopia. According to the book, the ideal society was to be made up entirely of free citizens who would elect their governing officials. Law would be enforced by citizens and not by the police. Money and greed would vanish, and everyone would practice a simple, ethical religion.

Italian painters of the late 1400s and early 1500s displayed such genius that this period is called High Renaissance. Leonardo da Vinci was a versatile man - artist, musician, architect, mathematician and scientist. He had drawn a human anatomical figure. He used mathematics to organize the space in his paintings. His most famous painting is the portrait called 'Mona Lisa'.

Around 1500 AD, many humanists suggested that the Church had lost sight of the spiritual mission proclaimed by Jesus. Church seemed more interested in its income than in salvation. In 1520, Martin Luther said that the sole authority was the Bible. Popes and Bishops could not tell a person what to believe. Ceremonies did not counteract sins. Therefore, priests had no role in helping people to salvation.

In the 1500s, scientists hoped to discover secrets of nature, such as why stones fall, why the stars seem to move, what are the functions of heart, etc. Success of these investigations in solving ancient problems in astronomy, physics and anatomy opened a new way of thinking that no longer relied on magic. The approach of experimentation was based on the principle that nothing was to be believed unless it could be proved. In the 1500s and 1600s, new instruments such as barometer, microscope, thermometer were invented that improved the ability to observe and measure.

In 1500s, a Pole named Nicholas Copernicus believed that the facts of astronomy were best explained by the heliocentric (sun centered) theory. In 1600s, Johann Kepler found that the orbits of earth and other planets moving around the sun are not circles, but ovals or ellipses. Galileo, an Italian professor of mathematics, made a telescope and showed that every heavenly body does not revolve around the earth. He proved mathematically that all the objects fall at the same speed in the absence of friction.

In 1687, Newton explained the laws of force and motion that control motion of planets. His law of universal gravitation stated that the force of gravity prevents objects from flying off the earth. A German mathematician, Leibniz developed calculus that studies continuously changing quantities. A Dutch scientist, Anton van Leeuwenhoek invented microscope in late 1500s that helped to discover bacteria and to observe a whole new world of life. Robert Hook of England also worked with microscope and was the first person to identify cells in living matter. Robert Boyle, an English scientist in late 1600s, worked out a basic principle describing gases and founded modern science of chemistry. A French scientist, Antoine Lavoisier demonstrated that matter can be neither created nor destroyed, but only changed from one form to another, which is known as the law of conservation of matter.

During 1700s, the idea that science does not accept anything as true that cannot be proved by mathematics and experiments became widely accepted. The thinkers of Enlightenment attempted to test everything by observation and determine the cause-effect relationship of natural events. Another characteristic of the thinking was rationalism, that is, the belief that truth can be arrived solely by reason. The thinkers of Enlightenment tried to apply scientific methods to examine critically the political and social institutions under which they lived.

2.9 Industrial Revolution

Industrial revolution began in eighteenth century when many new machines were invented to do the work that people were doing manually earlier. It brought a vast change in the way of production. The development was made possible by harnessing the usual sources of power such as animals, wind, and water more efficiently. A new source of power in the form of steam came into use.

Changes in agricultural production particularly in Great Britain assisted industrial development. Commercialization of farms and improved methods of agriculture helped to increase crop yields. New animal breeding practices resulted in more livestock production. Jethro Tull developed animal-driven machinery such as drill-plough to plant seeds in rows, break the ground and keep weeds under control. As a result of breeding advances and the increased availability of animal feed, meat production increased many-fold and meat became a regular part of diet.

The industrial revolution started in Great Britain because the country possessed all the factors of production - land, labour, capital, management, and a government to support all the activities. Cotton industry was the first to undergo mechanization with the loom for weaving using flying shuttle in 1733 followed by spinning jenny in 1764. Five years later, the machine was driven by water power. Richard Arkwright opened a spinning mill and employed hundreds of workers, beginning the modern factory system. In 1793, Eli Whitney invented the cotton gin that could remove the seeds to prepare cotton as fast as fifty people could do it with hand.

In 1760s James Watt, a Scottish engineer produced the modern steam engine and steam replaced water as the major source of power. Around 1850s, an American - William Kelly and an Englishman - Henry Bessemer discovered a new way of making steel called Bessemer process. It reduced the cost of production and steel became the basic material of industrial civilization.

Quickly the production of shoes, clothing, ammunition, furniture, printing, and paper making became mechanized. Invention of rubber and production of petroleum products further revolutionized the industry.

For centuries, goods of all kind had been produced by skilled artisans at small shops. Industrial revolution dramatically changed the way goods were produced and the way people lived their lives. In factories, workers concentrated on one particular task in the manufacturing process. This division of labour greatly increased production.

Rail-road era was launched in 1830 when Stephenson's engine opened the Liverpool and Manchester line, the first rail-road line specifically built for steam locomotive. Rail-road became essential mode of transportation and increased the demand for steel and coal.

In 1870s, a tremendous new source of power - electricity was developed. Electrical industry grew by leaps and bounds. Tremendous dams were built in many countries to provide this artificial source of water-power. Electric motors replaced steam engines in factories.

Invention of internal combustion engine that used a portable fuel supply of oil or gasoline started to propel individual vehicles called auto-mobiles. Motor vehicles and aeroplanes gave transport flexibility and speed not matched by horses and railways.

Industrial revolution resulted in corporations becoming the dominant form of business organization as new machinery required large amount of capital. Banks and other financial institutions played an important role in forming and operating these large corporations. Corporations at times joined together to avoid competition and created monopolies having complete control of a commodity or a service in a market.

Telecommunication changed faster than any other form of communication. Use of telephones expanded rapidly from 1880s. In 1920s, television was developed. Development of space programme after 1950s encouraged new form of electronic communication. Development of microchip opened up a new world of advanced communication. It allowed development of small and efficient computer systems, and a global telephone network. In the early 1990s, growth of Internet opened up a world of instant electronic information for its millions of users. The electronic communication and computers made offices and manufacturing automated.

Ever since the onset of large scale population growth and industrialization in 19th century, there has been a parallel rapid increase in man-made damage of the world's environment. Spread of industry after 1945 posed new threats to the environment. Acid rain from waste in the atmosphere destroyed forests and eroded buildings. Pollutants in rivers and seas poisoned aqua and wild life. High levels of carbon dioxide released from burning of fossil fuels raised global temperatures. Other chemicals began to weaken the ozone layer in the earth's atmosphere, which is responsible for reducing ultraviolet rays of the sun.

At Rio-de-Janeiro in 1992, agreements were made to reduce harmful pollutants and emissions. The richer countries subsidized industrial and agricultural projects in the developing world, which respected environmental guidelines.

2.10 World Wars

In 1914, most of the Europe was shaken by warfare. Expected to be short, the conflict became a long and bloody war, mobilizing civilians as well as soldiers and killing millions of people. By 1918, the war had become a global conflict.

Rivalries developed among nations in late 1800s both within Europe and overseas as a result of imperialism. The great powers built up their military strength and formed secret alliances to protect themselves. In the early 1900s, the imperialist nations came to the brink of war several times as they scrambled to partition Africa among themselves. In East Asia, the rival ambitions of Russia and Japan had already produced a war. Imperialistic rivalries in China continued to be dangerous to the peace. Weakness of the declining Ottoman Empire offered temptation to Great Britain, Russia, France, Austria and Italy, each eager for a share of the spoils.

Many European leaders believed that international problems could best be solved by the use of force. These nations in the late 1800s began to build reserve armies of men who were drafted, given military training, and then returned to civilian life. Armies increased in size, and large sums were spent on new weapons and for fortification of national boundaries.

Bismarck, the policy maker of German Empire, formed Triple Alliance with Austria-Hungary and Italy. The forging of Alliance isolated France. In 1894, France and Russia formed an alliance ending their isolation. As a result, Bismarck's great fear of facing potential enemies on two sides became a reality. Rapid growth of German navy troubled the British. In 1904, the British and the French reached an agreement over how to control Morocco and Egypt. With French help, an understanding was reached between Great Britain and Russia in 1907.

Archduke Ferdinand, heir to the Austrian Hapsburg throne, and his wife were assassinated by Serb nationalist in Sarajevo on 28 June, 1914. Austria-Hungary decided to punish Serbians for this outrage. German support for Austria and Russian support for Serbia created confrontation. When Austria invaded Serbia in July, the two European blocs found themselves fighting a major European war.

The war was fought between the Central Powers - Germany,

Austria-Hungary, Bulgaria and the Ottoman on one side and the Allies - the British, French, and Russians on the other side. Italy joined the allies in 1915. Romania, Greece and the United States of America also later joined them. Both sides had dug in along 650 kilometer front from the English Channel to Switzerland. Behind a tangle of barbed wire, machine guns and artillery, each side confronted the other for almost four years of fierce warfare.

Central powers were able to concentrate efforts on the western side with Russia's withdrawal from war after overthrow of Tsarist regime in a revolution in February, 1917. The German government authorized unrestricted submarine warfare to combat the Allied naval blockade. In April 1918, United States of America joined war on the Allied side that tilted the balance against the Central Powers. German forces broke through towards Paris until they were exhausted and became short of weapons. Allies pushed German and Austrian forces back in France and Italy. At the same time, things were going badly for Central Powers in the Middle East and the Balkans. Bulgaria surrendered first in September, 1918 followed by Turks. By November, a revolution in Austria-Hungary brought the old empire to an end. In Germany, the government of William II also fell as a result of war. A Republic was proclaimed, and two days later the war ended.

Costs of World War I staggered the imagination. Over 8 million people lost their lives in the battle. Many more were wounded and millions were crippled for life. For the first time in history, the loss of life among the civilian population was almost as huge as that among the armed forces. Naval blockades, artillery, aerial bombardments, famine, disease, and political violence all took their toll of life.

While treaty settlements were being worked out after the war, a special commission wrote the constitution of League of Nations. This convent was adopted by Paris conference and was included in Versailles Treaty. The League of Nations had two main aims. (i) To promote international cooperation. (ii) To maintain peace by the peaceful settlement of disputes and a reduction of armaments. It was to include all the sovereign nations.

By 1930s, the nations of the world were once again divided into opposing camps. One group included the nations satisfied with peace settlement of World War I, and the other group included dissatisfied nations. There were many local conflicts as a precursor of the World War II during 1939 to 1945.

Fascist Party led by Mussolini had risen to power in Italy in 1920s. In October 1935, Italy waged an all-out campaign to conquer and colonize Ethiopia, one of the few independent nations in Africa. The Rome-Berlin Axis was formed in 1936 and in the same year Mussolini declared Ethiopia as a part of Italian empire. Shortly afterwards, Japan and Germany pledged to work together to prevent the spread of Russian communism. It was soon endorsed by Italy.

In July 1937, Japanese armies captured Peking in China and began to move southward. China resisted the invasion, but its armies were inferior to those of Japan. By 1939, the Japanese occupied a fourth of China, including all its seaports.

By 1939, Nationalist forces in Spain defeated Loyalist troops in a civil war. Franco, the Nationalist leader, set up a fascist government modelled on Mussolini's dictatorship in Italy and became head of the state with unlimited powers.

In January 1933, Nazis under the leadership of Hitler came to power in Germany. Hitler was granted emergency powers to deal with any communist revolt. He used these powers to make himself a dictator. Liberals, socialists and communists were thrown into large prisons called concentration camps. In March 1938, Hitler proclaimed Austria as a part of German empire. In March 1939, Hitler sent his troops to Czechoslovakia and made it a German protectorate. The same year Mussolini invaded Albania on the east coast of Adriatic Sea. Italians won the country in a few days.

By the summer of 1939, British and French leaders could no longer maintain illusion about intentions of fascist dictators of

Italy and Germany. Britain signed a military alliance with Poland on 26 August, 1939. When Germany invaded Poland on first September, Britain and France declared war two days later. Poland was defeated within two weeks and was divided between Germany and the Soviet Union in an agreement in Moscow. Germany occupied Norway and on 10th May, 1940 invaded the Netherlands, Luxembourg, Belgium and France. In a time of six weeks, all of these were defeated. Italy invaded France, Egypt and Greece. German air forces tried to impose a surrender of Britain, which was repulsed and it was Hitler's first defeat. German invasion of Soviet Union began on 22 June, 1941 and German forces reached Leningrad and Moscow.

German victories prompted Japan to establish a new order in south-east Asia. On 7 December, 1941, Japanese planes attacked Unites States Pearl Harbor naval base in Hawaiian Islands crippling part of United States Pacific fleet. Japan then occupied colonial territories in South Burma, Malaya, Singapore, and the East Indies. Japanese attack brought United States fully into the war.

In January 1942, 26 nations met in Washington DC. These Allies led by Great Britain, Soviet Union, and United States pledged to use all resources to defeat the Axis. The Allies made available sufficient supplies to push Japanese from islands in the Pacific. Japanese forces were defeated in the Philippine sea in June, 1944. In March 1944, Japanese forces in Burma attacked India, but were defeated at Imphal. Japanese forces in the north fought both the Chinese Nationalists and the Communists. Between March to June 1945, Allied forces launched a series of devastating air attacks on 58 Japanese cities. Japanese sent suicide pilots to attack Allied shipping, damaging 402 ships. Decision to drop atomic bombs on Hiroshima and Nagasaki in August 1945 ended Japanese resistance. On 15 August, 1945, Japan surrendered unconditionally to the Allies.

Hitler's empire in Europe had reached its zenith in 1941.

Despite failure to defeat the USSR in 1941, Hitler declared war on the USA in December 1941. Allied cause was saved by a remarkable resurgence of USSR fighting power as well as by the prodigious manufacturing of American industry.

German rule was terrorist and exploitative. Millions of Europeans from France to Russia were taken as forced labour to Germany. Thousands were executed or imprisoned for their ideological beliefs. Around six million Jews were murdered in a state-sponsored campaign of genocide.

At the end of 1942, German forces suffered their defeat in North Africa and at Stalingrad in Russia. In July, 1943, the western Allies invaded Sicily in south of Italy while at Kursk on Russian Steppe, the largest battle was won by a well-organized Red Army. By 1944, Anglo-American forces had imposed crippling destruction on German population. It paved the way for massive Allied sea-borne invasion of northern France in June 1944, liberating it in four months. In April 1945, German Army in Italy surrendered. Italian guerrillas captured Mussolini and shot him dead. In 1945, a final assault on Germany brought Western and Soviet forces face to face across central Germany. On May 2, Berlin was captured two days after suicide by Hitler and German forces surrendered on 7th of May.

The World War II was enormously costly with loss of 55 million lives worldwide. After four years of destruction, Europe lay in ruin and its economy was shattered.

Plans for an international organization were discussed throughout World War II by the Allied leaders. By October 1945, required number of nations had ratified the Charter and United Nations was established. Member nations agreed to the following purposes of United Nations: (1) to maintain peace and security (2) to promote equal rights and the self-determination of people (3) to develop international cooperation and (4) to encourage respect for human rights and fundamental freedom without regard to race, sex, language, or religion.

Chapter-3: Evolution of Occupations

3.1 Introduction

Modern humans appeared in Africa about 130,000 years ago. Further expansion of human populations is evident about 50,000 years ago. By about 10,000 years earlier, humans had colonized almost whole of the habitable world. At the end of the last ice age 10,000 years ago, human population numbered only a few millions.

All the food for human consumption came from wild plants and animal hunting. Subsequently, people started domesticating some animal and plant species. Modern humans had learned to survive as foragers before start of agriculture. Humans moved seasonally in small groups to obtain their food supplies. Population densities remained low for a number of millennia.

The first occupation of human civilization was taming and domestication of different species of animals, which started at the time human-beings were wanderers or nomads before the Neolithic age (New Stone Age) 8000 years earlier. Some of the wanderers settled in villages at favourable sites. This change from wanderers to settlers led to the beginning of agriculture. This enabled more people to be supported on a given area of land at the cost of greater efforts needed to cultivate crops and raise domestic animals. Thus, raising crops for food and fibre was the occupation next.

Afterwards started the occupation of building houses for residential and food storage purposes. Agriculture and housing required tools made of wood and metal. The job of tool making started next. Irrigation of crops started the occupation of digging and maintaining canals and wells.

Before the advent of civilization, man performed natural task of gathering food essential to sustain life like any other animal species. As civilization advanced, new methods of gathering, hunting, production, consumption were developed. Subsequently, with settled life and complex civil rules, human-beings started developing specific skills to serve the society in a particular way. A system of payment of remuneration for an occupation started in the society. The remuneration received could be used to exchange goods and services produced by others.

Simultaneously, systems of governance and religion were taking shape. Some of the people with leadership qualities took to full time job of managing governance of common tasks. These people later transformed into kings and nobles. Kings maintained armies to save the community from external attacks by invaders from other communities. Religion also took shape with advancement of civilization with people starting to have faith in super natural powers in their day to day life. Some members of the society took to occupation of conducting rituals and other religious activities at the time of birth, marriage, death, etc.

Leaders in government and religion developed and interpreted code of conduct for members of the society. They developed calendar, which helped in timing of sowing and harvesting of crops. The same people invented writing in the form of pictures and sounds, which later developed into alphabets and written languages.

Humans were suffering from injuries due to hunting, fighting, accidents, natural calamities etc. Other health problems were also prevailing due to various forms of diseases, over-eating and tensions due to family and civilized life. Some members of the society explored use of certain plants and herbs for medicinal values, giving way to the occupation of physicians.

Some people started performing services to the society such as trading of animals and agricultural produce. Others started making yarn, cloths, shoes, utensils and other items of daily use. All these activities introduced newer occupations that people could take up to earn their livelihood.

When civilization was advancing, some members of the society did not obey the rules of the society. They wanted to disrupt order of the society by stealing hard-earned agricultural produce and belongings of other people. Some of them started using force to snatch earnings of others. They did not accept rules for sexual mating and marriage. They tried to practice forceful sexual activities. The society led by kings created police, jails and judiciary to control activities of these unruly people. Some members of the society took to the occupation of police, jail staff, clerks, judges, etc.

Kings and the members of the ruling class wanted resources to maintain army and common tasks of the society such as digging of canals, construction of roads, maintaining armies, policing, etc. They started collecting a part of agricultural produce as taxes. Some members of the society were employed for this job of collecting taxes for public expenditure.

3.2 List of Occupations

Newer technologies were developed with advancement of human civilization resulting in introduction of new goods and services in the society. It started introduction and evolution of newer occupations. The following sub-sections describe chronological development of prominent occupations after the beginning of human civilization.

Animal Rearing

Animal rearing for meat, milk, draft and wool have been part of the human civilization since its inception during Neolithic age. Goat, sheep, pig and cow species of animals were domesticated in the beginning in western Asia. This followed domestication of horses and camels for draft power. Other animal species such as buffalo, yak, poultry birds were domesticated in southern and eastern Asia.

Sumerian people developed dairy industry as early as 3000 BC. Cows were held in high esteem during early Vedic period in India during 1500 BC. Herds of cows were daily led to pastures for grazing. Milk formed an important part of diet in Vedic households. Sheep and goat were principle domestic animals in early Greek civilization during 1000 BC. Goat milk was used to make cheese.

Caring and treatment of the diseased animals created specific occupation in the society. A number of persons earned their remuneration by suggesting cure for livestock diseases. Trading of animals and organization of animal fairs has been practised since time immemorial. Animals were also used in sports.

People took to selective breeding of animals to obtain better quality and quantity of animal products. Peculiar animal breeds were developed for production of a particular class of products such as milk, meat, wool and draft power after years of selective breeding.

Livestock production and management has become mechanised today. Precision instruments are being developed for feeding and milking of animals. There is automation in the processes of slaughtering of animals for meat purpose. Packaging of meat and meat products is also mechanized. A number of dairy products such as ice-cream, cheese are produced and consumed in large quantities.

Newer methods of animal breeding that include progeny testing and DNA marker-based selection are being practised for improvement of animal production. Techniques such as artificial insemination are frequently used today. Technique of embryo transfer is performed by transplanting embryos from high-quality females into lower-quality surrogate mothers. This practice vastly increases the number of offspring, which may be produced by selection of the best quality parent animals. It improves the ability of animals to convert feed to meat, milk, or fibre more efficiently. These techniques are also used to improve the quality of the final product in terms of the desired content and taste.

Apart from livestock keepers, a number of persons are employed in animal product research and processing activities. Livestock farms employ a number of breeders, herd health specialists, feeders, and milkers.

Farming

Raising crops for food, fuel and fibre started with settled life of the human civilization. By 8000 BC, humans began to cultivate crops. By this time farming was well-established on the banks of Nile River. Growing dependence on agriculture led to increase in the number and size of settlements. Activity of agriculture is evident from the remains of wild plant species altered in morphology by human intervention. By the end of Neolithic age during 4000 BC, agriculture had spread from south-western area of the 'Fertile Crescent' to Europe, North Africa, Central Asia and South Asia. Agriculture began independently in China between 7000 and 6000 BC.

Grain crops such as wheat and barley, and fibre crops such as cotton were the first plants to be cultivated. Farming developed into a profession during 3000-1000 BC.

With enclosure movement of farms in England during 1600s and 1700s, scattered lands were combined to form larger farm holdings. This made it easier for farmers to experiment with alternative agricultural methods. Jethro Tull, one of the farmers in 1700s, invented a seed drill that enabled seeds to be planted in rows. New experiments showed that crops grew better if weeds were removed and soil between rows was broken. Crop rotation, the process of alternating crops of different kinds on a farm, helped in preserving soil fertility. The new agricultural techniques and machinery were expensive and farmers with small land holdings could not afford them. Also, fewer farm labourers were needed after introduction of machinery in farm operations.

Selection of crop varieties to produce better quality food and fibre has been practised since the beginning of crop cultivation. Farming has evolved into a complex profession in modern times. Today, it involves mechanised crop cultivation, pest control and post-harvest processing of farm produce. Thus, it has created many new occupations on the sideline. Biotechnological interventions have resulted in techniques such as tissue culture, and genetically modified varieties to produce pest resistance as well as food of desired contents of proteins, vitamins, and minerals.

As the agricultural technology advances, smaller proportion of population can produce sufficient food for human population. In the industrialized and developed nations, a small proportion of population is engaged in agricultural activities. Table 3.1 shows the proportion of population engaged in agriculture and allied activities in various countries. The underdeveloped country - Bangladesh employed 47.6% of the population in agriculture in the year 2010 while the developed countries like Germany and United Kingdom employed a little above one percent of their population in this occupation. Majority of the population in developed countries is employed in trade and services.

Fishing

Fishing is the activity of catching fish from sea and other water bodies for consumption purpose. It has been practised for 40,000 years. Fish has been a good source of food for people living

Table 3.1: Proportion of population (%) engaged in various occupations. Source: International Labour Organization, Department of Statistics Website.

Country	Year	Occupations		
		Agriculture	Manufact-uring	Trade and Services
Argentina	2014	2.0	12.7	73.0
Bangladesh	2010	47.6	12.4	35.6
Denmark	2014	2.4	11.8	78.1
Ethiopia	2013	72.7	4.5	19.9
Germany	2014	1.4	19.3	70.7
Iran	2010	19.2	17.0	48.5
Malaysia	2013	12.3	16.7	60.2
South Africa	2013	4.9	12.2	71.4
United Kingdom	2014	1.2	9.8	83.0

near sea and rivers. Archaeological features such as discarded fish bones and cave paintings show that sea food was important for the survival of humans. The Neolithic culture and technology spread worldwide between 6000 and 4000 BC when the new technologies of farming and pottery were introduced. At the same time, basic forms of the main fishing methods came into practice that are still being used. Egyptians invented various implements and methods for fishing and these are clearly illustrated in tomb scenes, drawings, and papyrus documents. Pictorial evidence of Roman fishing comes from mosaics which show fishing from boats with rod and line as well as using nets. In India, the Pandyas, a classical Dravidian Tamil kingdom, were known for pearl fishery as early as the first century BC. Their seaport Tuticorin was famous for deep sea pearl fishing.

Steam-powered fishing boats first appeared in 1870s that used the trawl system of fishing. These were large boats, usually 80 to 90 feet in length with a beam of around 20 feet. Fishing vessel as a boat or ship is used to catch fish in the sea, or on a lake or river. Many different kinds of vessels are used in commercial, artisanal and recreational fishing. According to the Food and Agriculture Organisation, in 2004 there were four million commercial fishing vessels.

Fishing industry includes any activity concerned with taking, culturing, processing, preserving, storing, transporting, marketing or selling fish or fish products. The commercial activity is aimed at delivery of fish and other seafood products for human consumption or for use as raw material in other industrial processes. Fishery management draws on fisheries science in order to find ways to protect resources so that sustainable exploitation of fishing is possible.

Fishing has evolved as an occupation with special class of people called fishermen. This occupation has become sophisticated today with use of advanced type of fishing boats and ships. Since World War II, radio navigation aids and fish finders have been widely used. Facilities of geographic positioning system, satellite tracking of fish are practised to pinpoint the catch in the sea. Fish farming in ponds has also been adopted as profitable occupation along with agriculture and animal husbandry.

According to Food and Agriculture Organisation statistics, the total number of commercial fishermen and fish farmers is estimated to be 38 million. Fisheries and aquaculture provide direct and indirect employment to over 500 million people in developing countries. In 2005, the worldwide per capita consumption of fish captured from wild fisheries was 14.4 kilograms, with an additional 7.4 kilograms harvested from fish farms (Source: https://en.wikipedia.org/wiki/Fishing).

Mining

Mining is the extraction of valuable minerals or other geological materials from the earth from an ore body, lode, vein, seam, or reef, which forms the mineralized package of economic interest to humans.

Since the beginning of civilization, people have used stone for tool making and ceramics for utensils. Later, metals were used to make early tools and weapons. Flint mines have been found in chalk areas where seams of the stone were followed underground by shafts and galleries. The mines at Grimes Graves are famous flint mines, which are Neolithic in origin.

Mining industry in the early Middle Ages was mainly focused on extraction of copper and iron. Other precious metals were also used mainly for gilding or coinage. Initially, a number of metals were obtained through open-pit mining, and ore was primarily extracted from shallow depths, rather than through the digging of deep mine shafts. Around 14th century, demand for weapons, armour, stirrups, and horseshoes greatly increased the demand for iron. Overwhelming dependency on iron for military purposes helped to spur increased iron production and extraction processes.

Today, mining operations can be grouped into five major categories in terms of their respective resources. These are oil and gas extraction, coal mining, metal ore mining, non-metallic mineral mining and quarrying, and mining support activities. Of all of these categories, oil and gas extraction remains one of the largest resources in terms of its global economic importance. A number of persons are employed in this occupation.

In the early 20th century, gold and silver rush to the western United States stimulated mining for base metals such as copper, lead, and iron. Canada's mining industry at Ontario was the major mineral producer of early 20th century with production of nickel, copper, and gold.

Australia by the 1850s was producing 40% of the world's

gold. In the early 21st century, Australia remains a major mineral producer. In the 21st century, globalization of mining industry of large multinational corporations arose. Peak minerals and environmental impacts have also become a concern. Different elements, particularly rare earth minerals, have begun to increase in demand as a result of new technologies.

Today, heavy machinery is used in mining to explore and develop sites, to remove ore stockpile, to break and remove rocks of various hardness and toughness, to process the ore, and to carry out reclamation projects after the mine is closed. Bulldozers, drills, explosives and trucks are all necessary for excavating the land. In the case of placer mining, unconsolidated gravel or alluvium is fed into machinery consisting of a hopper and a shaking screen, which frees the desired minerals from the waste gravel. Minerals are then concentrated using sluices or jigs.

Mineral processing is a specialized area in the science of metallurgy that studies mechanical means of crushing, grinding, and washing. Processing of ore from a lode mine, whether it is a surface or subsurface mine, requires that the rock ore be crushed and pulverized before the extraction of valuable minerals begins. After lode ore is crushed, recovery of minerals is done in combination of several mechanical and chemical techniques. All these mining processes employ millions of persons.

Trading

Some people started to work in the tasks other than farming such as making of tools, ornaments and weapons. Human societies produced food as well as some of the items such as clothes, tools, ornaments in access of their needs. There was exchange of the excess quantity of tools for food and other items within as well as across societies. Some people became merchants and traders who made their living by purchasing goods from farmers and artisans, and selling the goods to the needy at far away places. Thus, surplus production was transported to other civilizations in exchange for some other goods. This started an occupation of trading with full-time workers engaged in exchange of goods among societies.

Draft animals such as donkey, horse, and camel were used to transport goods from one place to the other. Boats and ships were built for trading through water ways and sea routes.

Long-range trade routes first appeared during 3000 BC. Materials used for creating jewellery were traded in Egypt since 3000 BC. Sumerians in Mesopotamia traded with the Harappan civilization of the Indus Valley. They also traded with other people of the ancient Middle East.

Egyptians were among the first people to build sea-going ships and sailed into the Mediterranean Sea. Trade was the most profitable activity during the Hellenistic world of Alexander. Arabs had long been traders. Goods from India and China were brought across the Indian Ocean to the Persian Gulf and the Red Sea. Then the goods were taken overland to Syria and Egypt.

Trade began to revive in Italy during 1000 AD after a lull during the Medieval feudal times. Goods from Asia were brought westward by Chinese and Muslim traders. The economic theory of mercantilism that advocated accumulation of wealth by a country encouraged collecting precious metals through trade. Nations tried to sell more goods in other countries than they bought, thus creating a favourable balance of trade. Colonialism played an important role in mercantilism during seventeenth and eighteenth centuries. Colonies producing gold and silver were the most desirable regions for control by Europeans. Next best were the colonies those produced raw material for industries in European countries.

After the industrial revolution in 1800s, goods had to be produced in large quantities to make production profitable with use of expensive machinery. People in Europe and the United States could not buy all the items being produced locally. Industrialists started looking for new markets in Asia, Africa and Latin America.

They wanted their governments to obtain guaranties for exclusive rights to sell in these markets.

Today, many independent nations have specialized in production of certain goods and services, which they export to other nations of the world. In return, they import a number of articles in demand in their countries. Internal and International trade is flourishing with modern production processes and advanced means of transportation. A number of goods introduced as late as nineteenth century such as crude oil have become major items in international trade. Trading of services such as finance, insurance, information technology have been introduced during twentieth century. It constitutes major portion of trade among modern societies. A large proportion of population all over the world is engaged in trading activities.

Politics

With the start of the civilization, humans had to collectively accomplish certain tasks of general welfare. Certain class of people with leadership qualities could manage cooperation among members of the society to accomplish common tasks, which included control over natural resources such as irrigation systems, grazing lands, common roads, etc. Cooperation was also required during natural calamities such as floods, droughts and earthquakes. External attacks from other civilizations required cooperative efforts of societies for their defense. Internally, some members of the society were defiant of the rules for food, sex and social order. It required a common system for enforcement of rules of the society including punishment for offenders.

The class of people having abilities to organise individuals and resources for common tasks became leaders of communities or tribes. Later, with advancement of civilizations and enlarged territories with city-states, they became kings, members of royal families and nobles. There was constant war among the kings of city-states to prove supremacy over others. Victorious kings established large empires.

Democratic Republics developed to manage societal common tasks as early as 1500-1000 BC during Vedic age in India. This was a form of government in which citizens took part to select leaders. Some of the Greek city-states around 500 BC developed democratic governments. Athens in Greece was a democratic state during fifth century BC. In some other Greek kingdoms, a council of citizens limited the powers of rulers. Early Romans set up a republic in which citizens entitled to vote chose representatives to run the government. In 27 BC, Augustus, the Roman Emperor became all powerful to rule the empire limiting the powers of elected persons.

Many forms of governments have been established during the course of history that included kingdoms, empires, feudalism, socialists and democratic systems of governance. Presently, most of the nations have democratic form of government where general elections are held at regular intervals. Politicians form political parties in modern democratic system and take part in elections. The political party winning majority of eligible votes forms the government. Many persons have taken up full-time occupation in politics. They organise and manage political parties, offer themselves for elections to hold government positions, and take part in framing laws and running the government.

Religious Activists

After start of settled life and civilization, human beings wanted to control everything surrounding them. But they could not control occurrence of diseases and natural calamities. Mourning at the time of death of family members and beloved were troublesome. Mysteries of origin of life and life after death were not resolved. There was confusion among the members of civilized society on the events beyond their control. This confusion resulted in people having faith in worshipping various tangible and intangible entities such as rivers, mountains, animals, etc. It resulted in start of primitive form of religion. Ceremonies during human life cycle, such as birth, marriage and death were performed with rituals and religious fervour.

Besides this, control on savages in the society was also a reason for beginning of the institution of religion. Political leaders framed certain rules in the society and defined penalties for those who did not obey the rules. But this was not sufficient to control uncivilized members of the society. Some leaders in the society framed rules for behaviour with other members of the society and described uncivilized actions as sin. Those who did not follow these rules were liable to be punished by super-natural powers.

Settled life created tensions among human beings regarding their family, occupation and social relations. Religious leaders defined certain activities including worship and ways to perform routines in human life so as to lead a peaceful and tension free life. Religion transformed people in general and powerful members of the society in particular to follow rules of the civilized society.

Emergence of modern religions such as Hinduism, Christianity, Islam, Buddhism, and Jainism further refined conductance of ceremonies and rituals. Some members of the society started performing rituals as full-time occupation for a fee, thus earning their remuneration from religious activities. These people working as priests were given different nomenclature in various religions. Religious workers also started managing houses of religion such as temples, for which they received remuneration. Priests performed role of teachers in earlier civilizations. They also helped in preparation of calendar and scientific innovations such as mathematical measurements, identification and cure for diseases, etc.

Religious activities have continued with greater fervour in modern times as well. Religious practices may include rituals, sermons, veneration (of a deity, gods, or goddesses), sacrifices, festivals, feasts, trances, initiations, funerary services, matrimonial services, meditation, prayer, music, art, dance, public service, or other aspects of human culture.

About 80% of the world population is affiliated with one of the largest religions, namely Christianity, Islam, Hinduism, and Buddhism. Members of various religions are building mega houses of worship. A number of people have adopted the role of religious preachers. Grand religious gatherings are organized where millions of people gather just because of their faith. Religious pilgrimage is preached as an essential activity during the lifetime of human beings. A large number of people are trained to perform religious activities, manage religious houses and organize religious gatherings. Thus, a number of people find occupation in religious activities all over the world.

Courts and Policing

Civilized society formulated laws to be followed by its members. The laws were enforced by a system of policing and judiciary. Offenders of laws were liable to be punished by putting them into jails. Every society had some kind of legal system and procedures to determine whether someone had violated a law. The law enforcement procedures provided employment to a number of people in the society.

Babylonian ruler Hammurabi during 1792 BC coded 282 laws to control all aspects of life - including property rights, contracts, bankruptcy, marriage and divorce. Laws were enforced by judges. In ancient Greece, judges interpreted the laws and applied them in each case. Courts in early Athens in Greece were democratic and jury of citizens formed the entire court. Under the Maurya administration in India during 300 BC, there were special tribunals of justice. Petty cases in villages were decided by headmen and village elders.

Law enforcement in ancient China was carried out by Prefects for thousands of years since it developed in both Chu and Jin kingdoms of Spring and Autumn period. In Jin kingdom, dozens of Prefects were spread across the state, each having limited authority and employment period. They were appointed by local magistrates who reported to higher authorities such as governors, who in turn were appointed by the emperor. Prefects oversaw civil administration in their area of jurisdiction. The concept of Prefecture system was also followed in other cultures such as Korea and Japan.

Roman judges had the belief that certain basic principles are common to all the humans. The Romans were among the first to use prisons as a form of punishment, rather than simply for detention. A variety of existing structures were used to house prisoners, such as metal cages, basements of public buildings, and quarries.

The first centrally-organised police force was created by the government of King Louis XIV in 1667 to police the city of Paris, the largest city in Europe at that time.

In Mogul administration in India during 16th and 17th centuries, officers called *Kotwals* were entrusted duties of policing in cities and towns. Their duties included patrolling the city to keep watch on law and order, and detention of thieves.

Industrial revolution attracted more people to live in cities from rural areas. In Great Britain, ten percent of people lived in cities in 1800. The figure was 80 percent by the year 1921. Governments of growing cities realized the need of a new kind of police force to patrol city streets to prevent robberies. The police was also needed to guide crowds during social and religious gatherings and to protect life and property of city people. In 1829, Sir Robert Peel, a member of British government, organized a permanent police force for London to maintain order and make sure that people obeyed the law. Other major cities soon established police forces.

Today, there exist special services for courts and police to enforce law and order in the society. Judges are employed in courts to listen and pronounce judgements in cases of conflicts as well as to decide on the quantum of punishment for law breakers. Those who are not satisfied with the judgement can seek justice in higher courts. A number of lawyers also find employment to put arguments in favour of cases of their clients. Courts keep records of cases that serve as guides for similar cases occurring at later time.

There are police stations in cities and towns, which maintain law and order in the society in their area of jurisdiction. They carry out criminal investigation and place the facts before the courts. The police is also assigned a number of other duties such as managing crowds on special religious gatherings, festivals, and helping people at the time of natural calamities.

Law offenders and punished persons are put in prisons for period of punishment announced in courts. Prisons are maintained by specific people employed under jail administration. A large number of people are employed in these occupations of police, jails and courts. In the United States of America alone, more than 74 billion dollars per year is spent on prisons, with over 800,000 persons employed in the prison management.

Artisans

Stone tools were made for hunting much before the start of the human civilization. Building of houses started with uncooked bricks. Later on, bricks were cooked in fire for building work. With invention of metals, tools and weapons were made of copper and alloys as early as 4000 BC. Wheel was invented during Neolithic age about 8000 years ago, which was followed by making of the wheel-cart. Likewise houses, palaces, temples, granaries, sewerage systems were built in ancient civilizations in Egypt and Indus-valley during 3000 BC. Jewellery was also made since the advent of the civilization.

Some people took to the profession of artisans to perform

different tasks of building work, making tools, utensils, jewellery and weapons. With time, these tasks of tool making became specialized that involved training and apprenticeship. Masters and apprentices manufactured different tools in shops during the middle ages from 800 AD to 1500 AD.

The Industrial revolution transformed the profession of artisans to automated manufacturing with power from water-mills and wind-mills during seventeenth century. Factories started running with division of manufacturing process into series of steps, and then assigned each step to a worker, constituting division of labour. Use of machinery aided the division of labour as machines performed many of the steps in manufacturing. Use of interchangeable parts of complex tools after 1900 made machines easily repairable. If a part of a machine was broken, it could be replaced by an identical part. Division of labour and the system of interchangeable parts made it possible to produce large number of items exactly similar in shape and size, leading to mass production. Assembly line by use of a conveyor belt that carried the unfinished products past each worker performing a specialized task saved time and energy.

During 20th century, new ideas and techniques dominated architecture. French architect Le-Corbusier was a pioneer in the use of rough-cast concrete. Architects also experimented with new ways of building houses. Standard housing units were cast in concrete and then shipped to the site. New plastic materials were also used in building work.

Today, fossil fuels and electricity drive different machines for tool making in factories. Production processes are automated with little intervention by workers. Robots are being used in manufacturing process to run repeated tasks. A significant proportion of the population is engaged as artisans in these factories. There are specialized occupations for building work such as architects, engineers and masons. A large number of unskilled workers are engaged as assistants and helpers to these specialized trained persons.

Textile

Human beings started covering their body with animal skin, tree skin, leaves, etc. It saved them from adverse weather. This was followed by cloth making from available natural fibres from plants and animal sources. Clothing was also required to cover the body in a civilized society. Wearing colourful clothes enhanced aesthetic value and demonstrated status of human beings in the society. Later, clothes made of fibres and wool were stitched according to the body shape.

Clothing also involved raising fibre-providing crops such as cotton and rearing of wool-providing animals such as sheep. Cotton was grown as early as 3000 B.C. Other fibres such as wool, silk were also used to make clothes during ancient times. Many people took to the job of spinners and weavers in textile industry as full time job. There were a number of tasks for production of fibre and stitching before delivery of final pieces of clothes. Lists of such jobs included yarn making from cotton, weaving the cloth, and tailoring the clothes to a particular body size.

The Industrial revolution during eighteenth century mechanized cotton textile industry that increased the production manifold. Textile industry was the first to undergo mechanization in England. Before the Industrial revolution, spinners and weavers worked from their homes to make clothes. With start of factory system, textiles were produced in spinning mills by employing hundreds of workers.

Today also, the textile industry employs a large proportion of population all over the world. In developing countries, it is the second largest employer after agriculture. Stitched clothes from developing countries are exported to high income countries of Europe and America.

Army / Fighters

Human-beings in a group attacked other civilized groups to gain access to resources such as fertile land, stored grains, livestock, pastures, etc. There was requirement of fighters to defend members of the society from such attacks. Fighters were also required to save belongings of people that had been earned and stored over time. Initially, all the members of a society fought to save their society from external attacks. A large proportion of the members of a society spared time from their main occupation such as farming and took part in fighting others. Over time, a class of fighters emerged who acquired specific fighting skills. They were also trained to use weapons in a war. Some of the fighters took full-time occupation in armed forces maintained by kings.

There is record of the earliest army organisations in India. One of the first known recorded battles, the Battle of the Ten Kings, happened when a Hindu king defeated an alliance of ten kings. During the Iron Age, the Maurya and Nanda Empires had large armies, the peak being approximately 639,100 soldiers.

Roman army had its origin in the citizen army of the Republic, which was staffed by citizens serving mandatory duty for Rome. In the earliest Middle Ages, it was the obligation of every aristocrat to respond to the call to battle with his own equipment, archers, and infantry.

Militarism became a belief of European leaders before World War-I during 1914-1918. European nations in the late 1800s began to build reserve armies of men who were given military training, and then returned to civilian life. Armies increased in size during the rule of fascist dictator Mussolini in Italy and Nazi dictator Hitler in Germany before World War II in 1939.

Sophisticated weapons have been developed for fighting wars in the modern world. Large countries employ millions of persons in their defence forces including army, air force and navy. Defence recruitments are conducted at young age. The recruits are trained to handle and use sophisticated weapons of war. Even in the advanced human civilization of the twenty-first century all the countries fear from external attacks. Some of the countries have to take up offensive against various fighters far away from their main land. These countries maintain their naval forces for ability to attack enemies in any part of the globe. A large number of persons all over the world are employed in this occupation.

Art and Dramatics

Man started painting caves during prehistoric times. Mural paintings in caves tell us about the artistic style of early Indian painters. Egyptians decorated their buildings with paintings 5000 years ago. With advancement of civilization, some people took to full-time professions of artistic activities such as paintings on pottery and walls, decorating buildings and public places, sculpture making, etc.

Renaissance in art during 1400 and 1500 AD was the greatest creative event. Princes provided jobs to many painters for making their portraits. Painters were engaged for decorating religious buildings, and palaces of kings and nobles.

Man had been performing mimicry and acting since the advent of the civilization. During the Golden Age of the Greek civilization in 400 BC, people started writing and performing dramas in poetic form. Ancient Greek comedy is traditionally divided between "old comedy" (5th century BC), "middle comedy" (4th century BC) and "new comedy" (late 4th century to 2nd century BC). Greek plays were performed in outdoor theatres.

Sanskrit theatre (Nātyaśāstra) is a compendium composed in India during 200 BC to 200 AD. The Treatise is the complete work of dramatic art in the ancient world. It addresses acting, dance, music, dramatic construction, architecture, costuming, make-up, props, the organisation of companies, the audience, competitions, and offers a mythological account of the origin of theatre. Indian drama developed greatly under Gupta Empire about 400 AD. It was performed in courtyards.

Great events of drama in England occurred in the 16th and 17th centuries. Many of the plays were written in verse. Shakespeare and other authors created historical plays celebrating lives of past kings, and enhancing the image of Tudor monarchy. Authors of this period drew some of their story lines from Greek and Roman mythologies or from the plays of eminent Roman playwrights.

Many persons took to the profession of acting and other jobs related to dramatics over history. Open theatre dramas are performed to this day with same fervour.

Invented around 1900, motion pictures swept through Europe and America. Earlier pictures were often simple dramas or comedies. In later film making after 1945, efforts were made to break traditional restrictions. By the 1980s, film making had become a major art form all around the world.

With advent of moving pictures in twentieth century, many new types of jobs were created in dramatics. There are thousands of people engaged in acting, photography, story writing, directing, producing, and distributing films. Some people are engaged as analysts, critics and commentators on drama and films.

Today, painters and artists get full time employment in film industry, construction, advertising, etc. Animation industry employs a number of artists to draw and print frames for animation dramas. Museums and art centres are built and people make payments to see the pieces of art. Paintings are sold and even auctioned in the open market.

Teaching and Philosophy

Informal methods of learning started with the start of the civilization where children acquired skills of performing certain tasks from parents. Formal education in Egypt was imparted in temples since 3000 BC. Likewise Sumerians usually organized schools in temples. There was a system of teaching in the schools of Gurus (called Gurukul) in ancient India.

Teaching of ethics, religion and language became a full time profession in Greek civilization during 1000 BC. Greek thinkers and philosophers - Socrates, Plato, and Aristotle started formal teaching in their schools during fifth century BC.

Main subjects of ancient philosophy were understanding the fundamental causes and principles of the universe. It involved the questions about things that cannot be perceived by the senses, such as numbers, elements, universe, and gods. Socrates is said to have been the initiator of more focused study on analysis of patterns of reasoning and argument, nature of good life and importance of understanding and knowledge in order to pursue it, the explication of the concept of justice, and its relation to various political systems.

Indian philosophy refers to several schools of philosophical thought that originated in the subcontinent. It included Hindu, Buddhist and Jain philosophies. All of these philosophies have common underlying themes of *Dharma* and *Karma*, and similarly attempt to explain the attainment of *Moksha* (liberation). They have been formalized and promulgated between 1000 BC to around 500 AD.

Some people took to the job of thinking and philosophy, which led to defining new rules for kings, nobles and general people in the society.

Philosophers explained working of mathematics and other scientific disciplines resulting in useful discoveries in science in Hellenistic Greek during 336-146 BC. Towns in Roman Empire had elementary and higher schools with Greek teachers. Nalanda was the chief centre of Indian education during Gupta period in 500 AD and it attracted students from Tibet, China and Korea. New schools were opened in prosperous towns in Europe during middle ages.

Teachers and students formed associations during middle

ages, which were called universities. Four great universities developed between 1000 and 1200 AD in Paris, Oxford, Bologna and Salerno. Over time, teaching became a profession and a good number of people were engaged in teaching in schools and universities.

Today, school education is freely imparted on government funding in almost all the countries of the world. There are a number of universities and institutes for higher learning and research in each country. A large number of persons are engaged in teaching and research. Equal number of persons is employed for administration and management of admissions, teaching, examinations, etc.

Health Services

The practice of taking care of health of human beings started before the start of the civilization. Humans found healing herbs to treat various wounds and diseases. Egyptians made discoveries in medicine during the period of old kingdom during 3000 BC. Early Egyptian books contain directions for setting fractures. In China, archaeological evidence of medicine dates back to the Bronze Age Shang Dynasty, which is based on tools presumed to have been used for surgery. Medical art of the Indus Valley civilization could distinguish a number of diseases.

Greeks were the first people to record their research so that it could be used later. Hellenistic age scientists added greatly to the knowledge of Greeks. Romans established a medical school in Egypt where Galen made studies that were used in Europe for the next 1300 years. Free hospitals were built in India during 400 AD during Gupta's rule. Susruta, a great Indian doctor, practised strict cleanliness before an operation and used to sterilize wounds.

In Middle East, the Arabs developed interest in medicine during 700 AD. At Baghdad in the early 900s, Rhazes wrote about surgery, diseases of eye, smallpox and measles. When the

Muslims invaded Spain, they brought medical knowledge to the Spanish universities. Monks in Italy had preserved the old medical knowledge, which combined with new learning in medicine was taught at Italian universities. Advances in medical science during the Industrial revolution were remarkable. During late 1860, French chemist Louis Pasteur learned that bacteria are responsible for many phenomena such as fermentation and causal of diseases in animals and humans. He developed a process of heating liquids to kill bacteria and prevent fermentation. He worked on producing vaccines consisting of weakened germs to prevent diseases like anthrax and rabies. An English surgeon, Joseph Lister developed antiseptic such as carbolic acid to kill germs causing infection during surgery. Causes of many other diseases such as malaria, yellow fever, bubonic plague were also explored. Alexander Flaming of Great Britain discovered the antibiotic penicillin in 1928, which came into wide use after 1940s. Antibiotics streptomycin was discovered in 1945. The antibiotics cured a number of diseases. The remarkable technique of X-ray photography allowed a doctor to diagnose a problem inside the body. These discoveries transformed hospitals from houses of death into houses of recoveries from diseases.

Today, there are a number of hospitals in each locality. Some hospitals are specialized to treat certain diseases such as heart diseases, eye diseases, cancer, etc. A large number of laboratories aid these hospitals in testing and diagnostics. Thousands of doctors, nurses, lab technicians, chemists find employment in imparting health services.

The system of medical education and training varies around the world. It typically involves entry level education at a university medical school, followed by a period of supervised practice or intern-ship, and residency. This can be followed by postgraduate vocational training. A variety of teaching methods have been employed in medical education, which are still a focus of active research.

In 1950s, structure of DNA (deoxyribonucleic acid) was discovered that is the basic component of genes and genomes. By understanding DNA, one can understand how genes and resultant traits are structured. This breakthrough made it possible to do research in viruses, bacteria, human cells and diseases like cancer. Modern biotechnology tools allow drugs targeted towards specific physiological processes to be developed, sometimes designed for compatibility with the body to reduce side-effects. Genomics and knowledge of human genetics have influence on medicine, as the causative genes of most of the genetic disorders have now been identified. It has initiated an era of drug designing and testing, which opens opportunities of employment for a large number of people.

Transportation

Transport of goods was an essential practice required for start of trade during ancient times. The first mode of transport involved walking and swimming by humans. Draft animals such as donkeys, horses were used for transportation in the beginning of the human civilization. Later, with the invention of wheel, goods were carried on horse-carts and bull-carts made of wood and metal. Boats and sailing ships were also used since time immemorial to carry goods through water ways and across seas.

The first forms of road transport involved horses domesticated during 4000 to 3000 BC or humans carrying goods over dirt tracks. Early civilizations such as Mesopotamia and the Indus-Valley constructed paved roads. Persian and Roman empires built stone-paved roads to allow armies to travel quickly. The Caliphate built tar-paved roads during the Medieval period.

Early water transport was accomplished with ships that were either rowed or used the wind for propulsion, or a combination of the two. The importance of water has led to growth of many cities as sites for trade being located on rivers or on the sea-shore, often at the intersection of two bodies of water.

The Industrial revolution during eighteenth century AD made better means of transportation necessary for carrying raw material to factories and finished products to markets. New ways of building metal roads were worked out. Steam engine made it possible to pull an assembly of cars and rail-lines were built to pull these cars. Steam ships were also developed that made transportation across oceans easier and faster than sailing ships. Many people were employed in various forms of transportation in all ages.

Invention of internal combustion engine using gasoline as fuel made it possible to move vehicles in late nineteenth century. It further revolutionized transportation on both land and water. Motorcars began to be manufactured in large numbers at the start of twentieth century. Invention of aeroplanes in 1903 made it possible to transport human-beings and goods through air routes.

Today, a good proportion of population is engaged in manufacturing, driving, maintenance, repair and other auxiliary jobs in transportation. All the historical means of transport are still in use. Goods are transported on horseback in hilly and difficult terrains. Horse carts are also in use in many parts of developing countries. At the same time, modern means of transport such as trucks, trains and aeroplanes are used for transport of goods from one part of the world to the other. Boats and ships have maintained their importance in bulk transport of grains, minerals, oil, etc.

Communication

History of communication dates back to pre-historic times, with significant changes in communication technologies over the course of the civilization. Human communication was revolutionized with the origin of language or speech approximately thousands of years ago. Symbols were developed about 30,000 years ago.

Pictograms were used by various ancient cultures all over the world around 8000 BC, when tokens marked with simple pictures began to be used to label basic farm produce. Invention of the first writing systems happened in the late Neolithic age during 4000 BC. The first writing system is generally believed to have been invented in pre-historic Sumer that developed into cuneiform by 2000 BC. Egyptian hieroglyphs and Indus-Valley script also date to this era. The Chinese script may have originated independently around the 1600 BC out of a late Neolithic Chinese system of proto-writing dating back to 6000 BC.

In the Middle Bronze Age, an alphabetic system is thought to have been developed in central Egypt around 1700 BC. Over the next five centuries, this Semitic alphabet seems to have spread north.

Communication through messengers has been practised since time immemorial. Greek historian Herodotus wrote about Persian mail service 2500 years earlier. Roman roads were used to carry messages from provinces to the capital. Marco Polo described a series of postal stations in China around 1300 AD.

With the invention of telegraph during mid-nineteenth century, communication across the globe became a reality. Wireless messages were sent through radio waves by the end of nineteenth century. Newer forms of communication started the business of telephony, which employed many people.

Invention of computers in mid-twentieth century made it possible to store and process information quickly. Computers helped in automation of factories, banks, transportation, communication, etc. Start of the Internet in the year 1992 has made it possible to share information over the globe at the click of a mouse.

Today, mobile phones and other communication devices have become essential part of day to day life. Many people are engaged in manufacturing of communication devices, software development, management of towers and services for mobile and

Internet uses. Communication has become real time with start of social websites.

In modern society, Information and Communication Technologies are omni-present, with over three billion people having access to the Internet. With approximately 8 out of 10 Internet users owning a smart-phone, information and data are increasing by leaps and bounds.

A large number of people are employed in development of computer hardware and software systems for automation and other uses of computing and mobile devices.

Electricity

Electricity remained an intellectual curiosity until 1600 AD, when the English scientist William Gilbert made a careful study of electricity and magnetism, distinguishing the lodestone effect from static electricity produced by rubbing amber. The English words "electric" and "electricity" made their first appearance in print in Thomas Browne's Pseudodoxia Epidemica of 1646. Benjamin Franklin conducted extensive research in electricity. In June 1752, he attached a metal key to the bottom of a dampened kite string and flew the kite in a storm-threatened sky. A succession of sparks jumping from the key to the back of his hand showed that lightning was electrical in nature.

Invention of electricity in 1870 AD, which could be produced by dynamo, revolutionized the lighting and clean power to industries. Electric bulb was invented in 1879 and after improvements it replaced gas light. Soon hydro and thermal power plants were started to produce electricity by running huge dynamos. Electricity from power source was transmitted to far away places through wires on poles. Industries started working on electric motor, replacing the steam engine.

A large number of people got employment in production, transmission, maintenance and supply of electricity. Similarly, employment was generated in production of electric bulbs, fans and home appliances. Newer sources of generation of electricity have been invented recently. Today, electricity is generated from wind turbines, solar modules, city waste and so on. Use of electricity has also become ubiquitous for home appliances, computers, lighting, entertainment, and factories.

Factory Owners and Managers

New machines were invented during 16th to 18th century AD for cotton textile, steel, printing, furniture, rubber, etc. These machines were powered by wind mills and water mills. Inventions of steam engine further revolutionized these industries. Power machines required huge investments and large organized working hands. Some people could manage capital for installation and operation of these machines under factory system. It started a new class of entrepreneurs who could arrange investments, finance and trained working persons for production of goods.

At the same time, some people were selected to supervise and manage the workforce, finances, raw material and finished products in a factory. They were called supervisors and managers. With time, the profession became more scientific and acquisition of relevant skills was important for aspirant managers. Today, managers are important people in all types of establishments engaged in production of goods and services. Specialized training programs are conducted to train managers to take up the task in various industries.

Money and Banking

Barter economy of exchanging goods and services was prevalent since the advent of the civilization where a person consumed the products produced by others in exchange for the products produced by its hard work. Many cultures around the world eventually developed use of commodity money. Mesopotamian shekel was a unit of weight, and relied on the mass of 160 grains of barley called Mesopotamia circa around 3000 BC. According to Herodotus, the Lydian were the first people to introduce use of gold and silver coins. First stamped coins were minted around 600 BC.

Money was used for facilitating exchange of goods and services since ancient times in different civilizations. The barter and primitive monetary system could not meet the demands of trade in middle ages during 1000 to 1500 AD. Money changers started banking services such as money lending and issuing special notes called letter of credit for trade. There was a great variety of money in use. Individual centres and cities made their own coins. There was no fixed standard for money.

Banking began with merchants of the ancient world who made loans to traders around 2000 BC in Assyria and Babylonia. In ancient Greece and during the Roman Empire, lenders based in temples made loans, accepted deposits and changed money. Ancient China and India also show evidence of money lending activity. The origins of modern banking can be traced to medieval and early Renaissance Italy, to the rich cities in the north like Florence, Lucca, Siena, Venice and Genoa. The earliest known state deposit bank, Bank of Saint George was founded in 1407 at Genoa, Italy.

In Europe, paper money was first introduced in Sweden in 1661. It reduced transport of gold and silver, and thus lowered the risks in trade. It enabled sale of stock in joint stock companies, and redemption of those shares in paper.

In the fifteenth century AD, Europeans began to develop standard system of money, which made transactions much more stable and reliable. This encouraged the growth of international commerce and rise of banks.

Modern banking practices emerged in the 17th and 18th centuries. Merchants started to store their gold with the goldsmiths of London who possessed private vaults and charged a fee for that service. In exchange for each deposit of precious metal, the goldsmiths issued receipts certifying the quantity and purity of the metal they held as bail. Gradually, the goldsmiths began to lend money on behalf of the depositor, which led to development of modern banking practices.

Napoleon established Bank of France under close supervision of the government. Bank reforms during industrialization led to creation of central banking system in 1844 in England. International Bank for Reconstruction and Development, often called the World Bank, was established after World War II to help finance rebuilding of war devastated areas and to help developing regions of the world.

Commercial bank money is created through fractional reserve ratio where banks keep only a fraction of their deposits in reserve while maintaining obligation to redeem all these deposits upon demand. Because of the banking practice, the total money supply is multiple of the amount of money created by the central bank.

Today, money is an important form of exchange for any type of internal and external trade among societies. Banking has become an essential part of modern civilization. Each nation has a Central Bank that regulates money and banking in the country. Banks also manage payments through credit cards and debit cards, commonly termed plastic money. Banks employ millions of persons to facilitate savings of individuals and firms as well as for lending for personal consumption and investment.

Stock and Shares

Merchants combined their resources and formed joint-stock companies for trade during the middle ages. Joint stock companies raised money by selling shares in the company to investors. Shareholders became joint owners of the company and profits were divided according to number of shares held in the company. Companies were able to raise large amounts of money for ventures such as exploration and trading.

The earliest recognized joint-stock company was the English East India Company. It was granted an English Royal Charter in December, 1600 with trade privileges in India. The Company transformed from a commercial trading venture to the one that virtually ruled India as it acquired auxiliary governmental and military functions. In 1602, Dutch East India Company issued the first shares that were traded on Amsterdam Stock Exchange. The Company became the first multinational corporation.

The innovation of joint ownership made a great deal of Europe's economic growth possible after Middle Ages. The technique of pooling capital to finance ventures such as building of ships made Netherlands a maritime superpower.

Large corporations were formed to invest in industrial organizations to produce and trade particular class of products. In these corporations, shareholders financial responsibility was limited to the amount invested. A large number of investors were attracted to the stocks of various corporations.

Over time, people started sale and purchase of shares in these companies in the open market. Individuals bought shares in companies and got powers to elect directors to decide policies of the companies. Stock exchanges were established to facilitate change of hands for shares of companies where many people found employment opportunities to broker sale and purchase of shares.

Today, there are a number of individuals and firms that maintain records of ownership of shares, facilitate trading of shares through stock exchanges and provide advisory services to investors. On-line trading of shares have become common with expansion of Internet facilities. A number of persons get employment in stock exchanges and related activities.

Sports

Human-beings spent their leisure time in playing some games, which developed into systematic sports over time. Sports in China appear to have started as early as 2000 BC. Gymnastics have been popular in China during ancient times. Monuments to the Pharaohs indicate that a number of sports such as swimming and fishing were well-developed and regulated thousands of years ago in ancient Egypt. Some sports that originated in ancient Persia are polo and jousting.

A wide range of sports were established in ancient Greece. Large stadiums were built in Greece 3000 years ago. First Olympic Games were held in 776 BC in the city of Olympia in Greece. Roman era also saw building of stadiums and organizing sport events.

During 1800s many games started to be organized formally. Football clubs for working people were created in 1850s. By the 1880s, players began to be hired as full athletes. Football became a sport played by professionals and watched by paying spectators. Olympic Games were revived during late 1800s.

In modern times, sports have become regular events with huge investments from governments and corporations. A large number of people are engaged in full-time sports activities. Many persons get employed as sports teachers, managers, coaches, doctors, commentators and so on. A larger number of people get employment in maintenance of stadiums.

Other Occupations

There are numerous other occupations providing employment opportunities to human beings in civilized society. Preliminary occupations such as retailing of goods, domestic services, personal assistance, security services, etc. have existed since the start of the civilization and are prevalent in the same form even today. Many persons find jobs in newspaper distribution, hotels, restaurants,

hair dressing, body-beauty shops, accounting, etc.
Numerous occupations that human beings can take with little training can be listed. Laundry services, hair cutting, shoe repair, tailors, plumbers, courier services, etc. are a few such occupations. Many innovations such as biotechnology, bio-informatics, drug design and testing have opened new avenues of employment. A number of persons acquire these specific skills in conducting scientific experiments and analysing data.

Computer software development has remained a manual task since its start in 1950s. Computerisation and automation of manufacturing and services have opened avenues of employment for millions with appropriate training.

Chapter-4: Categorization of Humans

4.1 Background

Human were born equal and lived as equals before the advent of the civilization. All the human beings had the same standard of living before development of the civilized society. They found food by hunting animals or by gathering fruits, nuts, grains, etc. Snatching of food from others must have been common among wild human-beings. There was no concept of clothes and everybody wandered naked without covering the body. Human-beings indulged in sex according to natural instinct and competitive power like wild animals. There were no rules for food, sex, fight, caring children, etc. Hence, there was no form of remunerative employment, family and society. Man was evolving with Darwin's theory of natural evolution, which states that the fittest individual have more chances of survival. Weak individuals are likely to die out and have less chance of reproducing their progeny.

As the civilization started and slowly matured into a civilized society, religious and civil rules were formulated. Now each member of the society was bound by rules to have food, sex and a status in the society. Everybody was required to work to produce food, and other goods and services for members of the society. A person received remuneration for the work that could be used to purchase its requirements of food, clothing, housing, etc. For fulfilling the desire for sex, each person was required to follow the rules framed for marriage and family.

Since the beginning of the civilization, there were majority of persons in the society who followed rules of a civilized society. At the same time, some persons could not follow the rules for food, sex, employment, etc. The situation is the same even after tens of thousands of years of the human civilization.

Human-beings can be categorized into four groups on the basis of their rationality, that is, the ability to follow the rules of civilized society, and organizational capabilities. This categorization implicitly includes causes for failure of human civilization to make each of the human beings follow the rules framed for creating a civilized society.

1. Type-I Rationals or Rational Organisers

2. Type-II Rationals or Rational Workers

3. Type-I Irrationals or Irrational Organisers

4. Type-II Irrationals or Irrational Workers

Typical characteristics of the four categories of persons are described in the following sections.

4.2 Type-I Rationals (Rational Organisers)

Type-I rational persons are organizers of political, religious, social and business activities of the civilized human society. These persons are leaders and role models in their domains. They formulate rules of civilized society in their domain of work. They generally follow these rules and make others to follow the rules of civilized society. Other members of the society look towards them for maintaining order in case of conflicts, natural calamities, external attacks, internal social disorders, etc. They possess the capacity to think and make appropriate decisions to save human-beings from going back to the savage and uncivilized life. They get remuneration for their job of management of affairs of the society, which is used for their consumption of goods and services available in the market.

These people enjoy high status in the society and have the power to fix their remuneration. Therefore, they form rich class of people in the society. They can take risk on their status and continuously make innovations in the field of their work for advancement of the society. Accordingly, their status in the society is also elevated with their successful tenures.

Various classes of people in this category are listed and described below.

Politicians

This class of people organize activities of common interest of members of the society. There has been a need for management of tasks of common interest to the society as a whole since the start of the civilization. The common tasks included irrigation facilities, mitigation of damage by natural calamities, internal social disorder due to conflicts on food and sexual relations, fighting external attacks, etc.

A few individuals organised members of the society to manage common tasks during the start of the civilization. They transformed into political leaders over time.

They were clan leaders during primitive stage of the civilization. They organized meetings of their clan members and framed rules. Members of the clan were required to follow the rules formulated by them. Offenders were liable for punishment such as bodily harm and curtailing right to resources. As different clans fought for supremacy and got amalgamated into kingdoms, Type-I rationals organized the kingdoms and took the title of kings. They organized armies to fight external attacks as well as for offensives against other kingdoms for further demonstration of their supremacy.

Policing was started by political leaders for internal security of people as well as to enforce contemporary laws. Judicial system was started for judgemental decisions on social and economic relations among people. Jails were built to punish offenders of the rules of civilized society. Jails were also utilized to keep savage members of the society confined so as to keep them away from disturbing order of the civilized society.

Kings also worked to organize irrigation facilities, land distribution for farming, road construction for transportation and trading of goods. They created currencies for smooth exchange of goods and services. Currencies were also used as the store of value for internal and external trade. All these activities of governance required resources in the hands of kings. Therefore, a system of taxation was evolved. Taxes started with transfer of a part of agricultural produce and income from trading activities to the common pool.

In modern times, most of the nations have democratic form of government. Politicians organize political parties and take part in elections to get elected to form government through general suffrage. Modern governments organize all the activities, which have been organized by kings during ancient times such as maintaining defence forces, internal social order, international relations, etc.

Besides the traditional activities, modern governments have taken much larger role with advancement of technology. Governments organize money and banking activities. They regulate investments, employment, education, health facilities, transportation, communication, etc. Even food distribution and housing are regulated and sometimes managed by governments.

Modern governments organize those businesses, which require huge investments. Some examples of these businesses are power generation, production of heavy machinery, mining, railways, airways, sea-ports construction, etc.

Religious leaders

All the human beings did not follow the rules defined by political leaders at the start of the civilization. Moreover, politicians were more concerned about retaining their control over the society and accordingly framed the rules. Rules for general behaviour could not be enforced by political leaders. Human beings were also concerned about consequences of their acts in life after death. Religious leaders came into picture to make rules for human life and death on the basis of facts around them. They have been organizing religious activities of the human society since time immemorial.

During ancient times, they formulated religious rules in the society that helped in converting human-beings into rational members of the society. These rules influenced behaviour of human beings at the time of eating meals, indulging in sexual relations, family life, and social involvements. They defined and interpreted rituals at the time of important events in life such as birth, marriage and death.

They established and managed common places of worship and other religious activities where people could gather to learn about religion. They tried to explain creation of the Universe, and mysteries before birth and after death, which influenced general behaviour of people. It also helped to mitigate worries of after-life.

Routine activities of human-beings in their family and occupational life created tensions and stress. This affected peaceful life and general health of people. Religious leaders searched ways to mitigate such tensions. They evolved methods of leading a peaceful life in the society. Postures for worship, yoga, and daily worship routines were the result of religious preaching.

Religious leaders made important discoveries in the course of the civilization. They developed calendars during early known history. A system of formal education was started by opening schools in temples. They acted as advisers to kings at the times of wars, internal disturbances and natural calamities. They also defined rules for the kings on general welfare activities.

Religious leaders in present times are organizing religious activities of societies like their predecessors. They preach their followers the ways to lead a peaceful life while maintaining their families and occupations. They organize large religious gatherings of followers where they teach them right ways of living a human life. People learn ethics from religion. Religious leaders form religious organizations for social upliftment of the followers. Doses of religious preaching are required continuously to maintain ethical human-civilization and mitigate stress of life in a civilized society.

Business leaders

With the start of settled life, there was need for exchange of surplus crop produce, animals and tools for specific products produced by other societies. Some of the Type-I rationals became business leaders to manage the trading activities. They collected surplus agricultural produce and tools for transport to faraway places. They could perceive demand for particular product in a society. Accordingly, the sale and purchase was managed by organising markets for the product.

Business leaders have been starting and managing business organizations to produce and trade products and services according to contemporary rules and permissions. They have been leading economic activities in the society during all ages of civilization. Business leaders can perceive demand for consumables in the society and start arranging raw material, capital and labour to produce relevant goods and services for consumption. They possess entrepreneurial qualities to start, maintain and advance business organizations.

During ancient times, business leaders organized hunting, fishing, food gathering, agriculture, textiles, tool-making and production of many items of daily use. They started trade through land routes on draft animals and carts. They managed to manufacture boats and ships to start trade through sea routes.

During modern times, the role of business leaders has become very important for the society due to mechanized production systems requiring huge investments and economies of scale to be competitive in the market. Modern business organizations require huge capital, land, trained workers and professional management. It is a Herculean task to start and manage modern businesses. Capital has to be arranged through issuing shares and bonds to investors. Additional funds are arranged through borrowing from banks and other financial institutions. Governmental regulations on capital, labour, and environment have become more and more stringent over time. Still, business leaders have the acumen to start and manage large business organizations on agriculture, banking, auto-mobiles, textiles, insurance, construction, etc.

Businesses can be organized on small scale also. The small scale businesses may involve small amount of capital and family labour. Machinery and labour can be hired at the time of need. Some examples of small businesses are agricultural farms, livestock and poultry farms, health centres, retail shops, repair shops for machinery and auto-mobiles, shoe making, etc. Whatever be the size of business, it involves risk of failure. Business leaders have the courage to take the risk and organise businesses of various scale.

With globalization of human politico-economic systems, business organisations are operating across international boundaries. International business arrangements have led to formation of multinational enterprises with a worldwide approach to markets and production of goods and services are managed accordingly. Most of the large corporations operate in multiple national markets. The new global marketplace requires companies to source goods, services, labour and materials overseas, and to continuously upgrade their products and technology in order to survive increased market competition.

4.3 Type-II Rationals (Rational Workers)

These persons acquire skills in performing a particular occupation through formal as well as informal training. After obtaining adequate level of skills, they find employment in the organizations started and managed by Type-I rationals. In this process, they earn their livelihood by receiving remuneration for their work. They spend their earnings to consume goods and services available in the market. This category of human beings can be called Rational Workers because they act according to the rules of civilized society to earn their livelihood from the work permitted in civilized society, and maintain their life peacefully according to the prevalent rules.

During ancient times, human-beings received informal training while helping their parents in doing various tasks in agriculture, animal husbandry, tool-making, artistry, trading, armed fighting skills, etc. Over time, formal systems of education and training developed. Young persons were admitted as apprentice in a business organization where they developed their skills in production of a particular type of product or service. Now-a-days, formal system of education and training has developed in almost all the spheres of production systems for various goods and services.

All the persons performing various socially-accepted occupations are included in this category. People get training in various occupations to get employment in respective organizations. Some people acquire skills in agricultural operations like raising crops, horticulture, animal husbandry, fishery, etc. and get employed by people owning and managing agricultural farms. Some persons receive higher education in a particular field of study and become teachers in schools and colleges. Some people are trained in various systems of medicine and become doctors in hospitals. Some people are trained in doing research for solving problems of a particular business and are employed as scientists in research and development organizations. Those who study prevalent law in the society get employment as lawyers and judges in courts. Engineers take jobs in construction and manufacturing activities. Technicians in different trades do various operational jobs in relevant organizations. Managers arrange day-to-day operational activities in running business organizations. Musicians and actors find work in drama and films. Some persons receive training in performing religious activities and get employed in religious organisations.

Some people join defence forces of their country and obtain training in performing duties in external security of the society. Some persons join police services and get trained in law enforcement to maintain internal security of the society. Other people find employment in banking and become expert in management of savings, loans, currency and other banking operations. A number of individuals join political parties and social organisations as full-time workers.

Many persons get on-job training and acquire skills after completing formal education in schools and colleges. They are promoted due to their further training and experience. Some people shift occupations due to newly acquired skills.

Some people belonging to this category do not acquire much education and training. Still, they find employment as helpers and assistants in various domestic and commercial activities. Over-time they develop their niche in the job through sincerity and dedication in their duties. They earn reputation of sincerity in their duties and are in demand among employers. Thus, they command good remuneration. For example, a good domestic helper is always in demand in the neighbourhood.

Rational workers find some employment and earn their livelihood in an easy and natural way as per rules of the society. They are generally well-off people and form middle and high middle income group in a civilized society. Some of them can receive very high remuneration due to their niche skills acquired over time due to natural talent and hard work. For example, some film actors earn very high amounts of money as fees due to their accepted acting styles. Likewise, some sports persons, lawyers, doctors, scientists, accountants have very high levels of income due to high demand for their skills.

4.4 Type-I Irrationals (Irrational Organisers)

These persons possess the capacity to organise but they do not follow rules of civilized human society. They organize anti-social activities - the activities which are not permitted under rules of the society. This category of people can also be called Irrational Organizers.

During ancient times, these people organized gangs to spoil establishments of civilized society. They did not take part in social and economic activities such as hunting, food gathering, agriculture, animal husbandry, tool-making, etc. Rather, they attacked people of the civilized society to loot all the gains of hard work of other members of the society, such as food, clothing, livestock and other belongings.

This category of people did not follow the rules for sex and family life in the society. They tried sexual indulgence forcibly against the wishes of their mate. They did not have any family life and lived isolated from social establishments.

Civilized society mobilized resources to engage some of its rational members to fight these persons in case of attacks on their earned belongings. The fighting between rational and irrational humans disturbed peace in the society. In general, power of rational persons remained strong due to willingness of human beings to live in peace and order as savage life could push them back to the living in wild form. Irrational organisers were caught and punished. Alternately, they were made to hide in remote areas away from human settlements such as forests and hills. This arrangement of fighting irrational organisers has matured into policing in today's civilized society.

In modern times, this category of persons organize many illegal activities. They organise smuggling of goods and services to evade taxes. Production of prohibited goods and services is also organized by them. Many criminal activities, which they organize include prostitution, food adulteration, drug trafficking, kidnapping for extortion money, organized begging, terrorism, etc.

This category of people are generally rich as they make quick money by indulging in illegal and anti-social activities. But they cannot lead a peaceful life. They have to live in hiding most of the time. So, they cannot make use of their possessed resources in the way rational members of the society spend their income on comfortable housing and other amenities. Secret agents and police of the civilized society are always there to nab them and bring them before law of the land. They are put in jail and criminal cases are initiated against them. They are punished by courts of law in the form of monetary fines, confiscation of property, imprisonment and even death sentence. In case they evade police, they are chased and killed. Civilized society feels proud of their police when these people are put to justice. Police personnel get rewarded for the bravery to bring these people to justice under the rules of society.

4.5 Type-II Irrationals (Irrational Workers)

Persons in this category cannot find work according to their abilities, and as per rules of civilized society. This category of people can also be called Irrational Workers.

Civilized society wanted each of its members to get engaged in production of goods and services that are useful for human-beings according to the permitted rules. Some persons could not adjust to the rules of the civilized society at the time of formation of the civilization. They could not perceive demand for any product, in which there was possibility of getting training and subsequently employment for them. They were generally not employed in any of the permitted occupations. They remained unemployed for most part of their life-span. Thus, they formed poor people in the society. Some of the irrational workers became prey to irrational organizers in the society and took part in organisations involved in restricted activities. The process is still continuing and a good proportion of people in various societies fall under this category.

Type-II irrationals can be further categorized into irrational followers and irrational offenders on the basis of their belief in rules of the civilized society. Typical characteristics of these subcategories are described in the following subsections.

4.5.1 Irrational Followers

This category of people believe in civilized human society. They want to work according to the rules of society. But they are not serious to receive training in a particular occupation. So, they cannot find continuous employment. They remain poor due to inadequate remuneration earned by them because of loss of employment time and again. Therefore, they cannot purchase all the necessities of life such as food, clothing, housing, etc., making their life miserable in the society. Despite the miserable condition of their life, they do not try to receive training in performing jobs, which are in demand at the time or in near future.

Successful employment in various occupations requires a set of behaviours in the civilized society. But this category of persons does not behave according to requirement of their job and therefore they are out of work. For example, a salesperson should always be polite to customers. In case of undesired harsh behaviour, a salesperson will be removed from job by the employer.

At times, this category of persons might earn more than sufficient remuneration out of their hard work. But they are ignorant of spending their income judiciously so as to draw maximum satisfaction out of it. For example, they might spend their income on parties and merry-making rather than spending it on education of their children. Either they have no intention to save part of their income for future needs or they lack knowledge about safe avenues of putting their savings.

Some persons in this category of irrational followers during start of the civilization might have started begging to get minimum requirements of food and clothing, which was permitted by the society. Every religion advocated helping beggars. Kings distributed alms to beggars on special occasions. But beggars could not get any status in the civilized society. They remained poor but lived in peace and harmony in the society. Even if they could collect sufficient alms while begging, their condition remained miserable.

Modern welfare governments arrange food, housing and health facilities for this category of persons. They remain satisfied with meagre aid of resources. They become habitual of aid by governments and rich people. Therefore, they always think ways of receiving alms and cannot think about doing anything challenging in the society. So they keep a low status in their life.

4.5.2 Irrational Offenders

At the start of the civilization, some persons in the category of the Type-II Irrationals came under influence of Type-I Irrationals who could organize anti-social activities in the civilized society. The logic put forward for indulging in undesired activities could be assumed injustice done to them by those who had become rich by controlling resources such as agricultural land and livestock in the course of civilization. Thus, Irrational Offenders started unlawful work under the leadership of Irrational Organizers. At the same time, irrational organizers could find necessary manpower to organize illegal activities in the society.

The chain of existence of irrational offenders still continues in the society. They are swayed by cunning and dishonest leaders because of negative thoughts about the civilized society. They indulge in illegal activities like theft, looting, sex crimes, drug trafficking, money laundering, etc. Sometimes they are lured into terrorist activities in the society in the garb of religion, regionalism and ideological rumblings. At times, they have even been lured to act as suicidal killers by irrational organizers in the garb of injustice due to politics, region, religion, poverty, etc.

Anti-social irrational workers may earn good money by doing illegal activities, but their families remain poor. Most of the time, these people are caught, put to justice and have to remain in jails. They carry the risk of being killed in encounters with the police. Their children are also vulnerable due to lack of formal education, training, and resources making them poor for their lifetime. Many of their children also grow as Type-II Irrationals due to their learning in an anti-social environment.

4.6 Change of Categories

Nobody is born in a particular category of human beings in the society. All the human beings are born equal at the time of their birth. People acquire characteristics of a category from their family background and neighbourhood. Teachings during early life also help in pushing a person to a category of human beings. Many persons change their categories over lifetime due to social environment or formal and informal learning.

Human-beings have strong desire to pass on their legacy to their off-springs. Therefore, the society has permitted to pass-on the earned and saved property to children after death of parents. Rational organizers are rich people and their children inherit huge property such as land, money, status, religious establishments and business organizations. Children also acquire social behaviour to manage the inherited property from their parents. Most of the persons can manage their inheritance well and remain rational organizers during their life-time.

Some people become speculative and careless about managing their property. For example, a person inheriting a well-managed textile factory may start gambling in horse-racing, future stock trading, speculative transactions in immovable property, etc. In the process, he may incur losses much beyond the value of his inherited factory. He might have borrowed from banks and other financiers for investments in speculative activities. But he may not have the capacity to repay these loans. Financiers will ultimately dispose off his inherited factory to recover their money. Thus, the person may lose property and status over time. Ultimately, such losers have to move to the category of rational workers in one or more generations.

Some of the rational organizers indulge in activities that are not permitted in a civilized society. They start violation of rules to upkeep their status in competition to other people of their category. This may include tax evasion, smuggling, hiring of illegal labour, hiding of finer details of products, etc. Due to continuous involvement in organising illegal activities, they might move to the category of irrational organizers over time.

Rational workers educate and train their children to take up jobs in political, religious and business organizations. Some of the rational workers or their children learn and develop entrepreneurial skills. They take initiatives and build firms that hire professionals from various fields, and thus they move to the class of rational organizers. There are many examples of such people in the past as well as in the present society. Napoleon, a soldier in French Army, organized armies to win wars. He became king after winning a few wars during the last decade of 18th century. Now-a-days, many professionally-trained managers, engineers, doctors start business organizations in their field of expertise. They provide employment to a number of other persons in the society.

Falling prey to favours and corrupt practices has been a major problem with rational organizers as well as with rational workers. Persons of both of these categories continue to perform their duties, but they begin to violate rules of the society by favouring their family members and relatives. At the same time, they violate rules for monetary gains from some people for illegal favours. These corrupt practices create mistrust in the society, leading to more people violating rules of the society. Ultimately, this causes some people moving to categories of irrational organizers and irrational workers.

Some of the irrational followers fall prey to irrationals organizers in the society and move to the category of irrational offenders. A few reasons for this shift in category can be listed as greed for money, passion for sex, religious fanaticism, regionalism, etc.

Sometimes, irrational organizers are influenced by preaching of rational organizers, particularly of the religious leaders. As a result they move to the category of rational workers or even to the category of rational organizers after obtaining appropriate training.

Irrational workers move to the category of rational workers under the influence of rational persons in the society who make them understand the value of education and training. They are brought to the point that there is ample number of jobs available in permitted occupations. They obtain appropriate training and skills and get employed in various occupations in the society. This also includes behavioural training required in performing a particular kind of work.

Likewise, irrational offenders indulged in anti-social activities move to the category of rational workers after being jailed for a few years. Jail officials arrange for their training to perform useful work for the society. Rational organizers are invited in jails to preach the benefits of following obedient life in a civilized society. They may understand the preaching of rational people, particularly religious leaders, in the society and get involved in socially-accepted jobs after their release from jail.

4.7 Basis of Categorization

The above categorization of human-beings in a civilized society is mainly based on psychological personality disorders. In turn, personality disorders are the result of injustice in a civilized society.

Personality disorders are deeply ingrained habits or patterns of behaviour of humans (Nathan & Harris 1980). Persons with personality disorders are not solely bothered by their troubling behaviour, it can even disturb others. They show little flexibility in approaching an acceptable life. Various types of personality disorders and their typical characteristics are listed in the appendix- B.

When we read about different types of personality disorders, the categorization of human beings on the basis of rationality is revealed in our minds. Although personality disorders cause people to belong to irrationality in the society, some disorders might make people to perform a particular class of task better than others.

There can be the following two intertwined considerations to derive human beings to various personality disorders and hence various categories of human beings appear.

1. Environmental factors

These factors include family and social environments. Most of the adults with anti-social personality disorder come from homes where the father is psychopathic, alcoholic or where the family is broken by separation or divorce (Nathan & Harris 1980). A child in a happy and stable family has favourable conditions for personality development that help in its future adjustment to the society (Rees 1982).

A society with irrational organizers becoming political, religious and business leaders induce irrationality in the society. During ancient days, kings used to create irrational social environment particularly after winning the wars. They used to inflict atrocities on losers, thus pushing them towards irrationality. Many of the modern governments are functioning under democratic set-up. But political leaders indulge in favours and many other corrupt practices. This creates a social environment that creates overall irrationality in the society. People in this environment fail to trust others and play mischief in all their economic and social activities.

2. Path dependence

What path we take in life is driven by behaviour of our parents and forefathers. The basis of path dependence for categorisation has been adopted from the book by Beattie (2009). An example has been quoted in the book on why pandas are so useless that they need conservation while cats have survived along human civilization. Pandas have biological problems of consuming and reproducing, making them vulnerable. Pandas eat bamboo, which is low in nutrients. They are bad in mating. Cats have merged with humans by becoming pets. Domestic cats are highly efficient hunters and eat a wide variety of foods. They breed easily. Therefore, cats do not require any conservation efforts.

Societies (including families and persons) choose their path and the path chosen in the past may make it hard to plump for the right option in the present day. Path dependence resembles evolutionary biology - the role played by a sequence of events, some of which may come by chance. A change in direction requires large amounts of courage, luck and strength to find a better path.

The path taken by human-beings has been of fighting, wars and atrocities on the opponents. Defeated groups and societies were suppressed brutally in history. Over the years, these suppressed people developed slave psychology of not taking any initiatives on their own. These people become Type-II rationals who try to find employment in established organisations. Many of them transform into the category of Type-II irrationals who either remain without job or fall prey to anti-social people. This is still happening within and across societies.

Chapter-5: Employment

5.1 Introduction

Before the beginning of civilization, human-beings were engaged in hunting and gathering to fulfil requirement of food. Storing food from activities of gathering started with the advent of the civilization. Subsequently, cultivation of crops for food was initiated. Over the course of the civilization, humans started living in clusters. Housing activities started with settled life. Humans started covering their body with animal and plant skins. This gave rise to need for clothing. All these activities required tools and implements. People started making tools for agriculture, housing and clothing. The leisure time due to settled life was spent on artwork.

All these tasks of civilized society could not be performed by a person or a group of persons alone. Persons took specialized tasks to produce a particular type of product such as food, clothing, housing, tools and other items. They could exchange their earned items with other members of the society for the items that they did not produce. Members of the society started exchanging stored grains, clothing, housing, tools, etc. to fulfil requirements of products and services produced by others. In this way trading of goods started in the human civilization. Demand for the items produced by other societies resulted into trade among various societies and civilizations.

A person was required to learn skills to produce a particular class of permitted items. By producing these items, it was able to command value from the demand for items in its possession. This enabled people to engage in remunerative employment.

Employment of a person in the society means that he or she is engaged in producing goods or services, which are permitted by rules of a civilised society. In return, the person gets remuneration that is used to purchase goods and services available in the market for its consumption. Production of a number of goods and services are not permitted in a civilized society. For example, cultivation of poppy and production of opium is not permitted in many societies. Likewise, indulging in sex for a price is prohibited in general. Engagement in these prohibited tasks cannot be termed as employment. In the same way, activities of theft, looting, extortion, etc. are not termed as employment.

In primitive societies, there were small numbers of occupations such as agriculture, animal husbandry, tool-making, food gathering and hunting where people could get employment. Various occupations were added during advancement of the civilization, which included carpentry, mining, health services, defence services, transportation services, entertainment, etc. In the modern society, many more occupations are available that a person can take up to earn remuneration. Some examples of modern occupations are education services, computer services, travel services, wealth management, media services, and so on. Domestic and other help services have been practised since ages and are still in demand in all the societies.

Taking up employment in the society requires a person to acquire skills to perform certain type of jobs. Skills can be learned through formal or informal education while a person is growing from childhood to adulthood. Each member of the society is required to learn and develop certain skills, and use them for production of goods and services for consumption by other members of the society. This enables people to find employment in the society and earn remuneration to buy goods and services available in the market. Individuals with little or no skills also find work as domestic and office help in cleaning, sweeping, etc.

In a nutshell, each member of the society should be engaged in producing certain goods and services that are permitted and are in demand. Each person has been blessed with sufficient physical strength and intelligence level to acquire one or the other skill. Therefore, theoretically, every person should be employed in a society at every stage of the civilization. This implies cent percent employment at all stages of the civilization. As the civilization advances with newer technologies and machinery, goods and services are produced at greater speed in more quantity as well as of superior quality. More and more products and services produced with better speed are available in the market with mechanized production systems. Thus, human beings enjoy better living standards and more leisure time with advancement of technology. It should not affect the level of employment in the society. There should be a state of full employment at any level of technology.

An example of technology-led production, consumption and employment can be given on invention of auto-mobiles at the start of the twentieth century. Before invention of auto-mobiles, animals and animal-pulled carts were used to transport persons and goods from one place to the other. Many persons were employed as carters. A large number of persons were employed in manufacturing of carts from wood and metal, repair of carts, breeding and keeping of animals such as horses to pull carts, etc. Auto-mobiles replaced these jobs leading to different categories of work such as drivers, manufacture of cars and trucks, repair of auto-mobiles, etc. This invention provided humans with speedy and comfortable means of transportation. Also, many more people could afford to travel and transport goods using one or the other form of auto-mobiles. The level of employment in transport services remained the same even after the invention. Only the quantity and quality of transport improved with the invention.

The state of full employment can be illustrated through a hypothetical example. Let us consider a population consisting of 1000 persons living in a locality. The society is fully employed with every member of the society employed in one or other occupation of providing food, clothes, housing, transport, communication, trading, domestic help, etc. Suddenly 500 more persons join the population through migration and now the locality has a population of 1500. The additional population also requires food, clothing, housing, education for children, health services, transportation, retail services, etc. At the same time, these persons have to get employment so that they are able to earn remuneration to pay for the purchase of all these goods and services for consumption. Over a little gap of time, the additional population will intermingle with the original population in terms of production of goods and services. At the same time, they will consume goods and services produced in the society, thus creating additional demand. There will be requirement of persons for the additional food production, housing, schools, hospitals, retail shops, telecommunication, clothing, religious services, etc. To fulfil the additional demand for goods and services, the migrated persons will take up different occupations and start serving the society in the same way as the original 1000 persons were serving before the migration. In case they bring new skills with them, the original population will also consume products of their new skills to enjoy better standards of living. In the same way, the new entrants will enjoy products of all the skills possessed by the original population.

Full employment in the society is a universal fact despite availability of space and natural resources remaining constant even after increase in the population. A crowded locality may outsource production of a few goods to other localities. This is happening with large cities that outsource food production to far away rural areas. In turn, people in these cities produce industrial goods and administrative and financial services for the population living in villages.

But practically a small portion of population has remained unemployed in all the societies at all the stages of civilization. The problem of unemployment is more visible in modern industrialised society. Some persons including elders who have saved enough money during their active lifetime may be without work. Pensioners are also not engaged in any work. These people are not counted among the unemployed. Only those with involuntary and chronic unemployment are counted as persons without a job. Various economic theories explain existence of unemployment in the society.

5.2 Theories on Employment

Classical theory of employment

Classical theory of employment assumes that there is always a state of full employment in the society due to forces of free market. The situation of free play of market brings about utilization of all the existing labour into gainful employment. It adjusts demand and supply of labour to the state of equilibrium where the demand and supply of labour becomes equal. Interference with the free play of market forces restricts to bring about full employment. Therefore, if the goal of full employment is to be achieved, government forces should not interfere in the freedom of economic forces of demand and supply.

The classical theory is governed by Say's Law of Markets, which narrates that general overproduction and unemployment are logical impossibilities. French economist J. B. Say's famous statement goes "supply always creates its own demand". It is the production, which creates its own demand. Any new production of goods creates its demand on account of payment of remuneration to factors of production during the production process. It creates equivalent amount of purchasing power in circulation that leads to sale of the product in the market. For example, manufacturing of motor-car also brings an equivalent amount of purchasing power in the form of wages, profits, interest, etc., which might be used for purchase of the motor-car along with other products. In this way, if general overproduction is impossible, general unemployment is also impossible.

Classical economists accept certain portion as voluntary unemployment when people do not want to work, and frictional unemployment when people are in the process of shifting jobs. However, in reality there exists involuntary unemployment in the society. There are persons in the society who remain unemployed, although they are willing to work. According to classical economists, such unemployment is due to interferences with the free working of economic system, which may be due to demands from trade unions, government intervention on minimum wages, etc. Prof. Pigou, the great classical economist, argues that the removal of interferences and existence of free competition would force the wages down until it is profitable for employers to engage everyone willing to work. The existence of unemployment is due to rigidity of wages. Employment of idle persons or resources shall pay itself, as they help in increasing the production of a volume of goods and services in the society. The size of income increases with employment of persons and resources that can be used to pay remuneration to the newly employed persons. The economic system works itself without any external stimulus.

Say's Law of markets has been criticized from two points of view. Firstly, the supply of goods does not create its own demand. The fact is that people do not spend their entire income and save a part of the income for future use. This reduces the present demand for goods and services. Secondly, the supply of labour does not automatically adjust itself to its demand. This is evident from the existence of unemployment in almost all the countries. Even a reduction of wages does not cure the problem of unemployment.

Keynesian theory of employment

Lord Keynes during nineteen thirties put forward a systematic theory of employment, which is often referred to as the demand deficiency theory. It attributes unemployment to lack of effective demand in an economy leading to deficiency of outlay on consumption as well as on investment.

Effective demand comprises of the demand for consumption of goods and services, and the demand for investment on capital goods such as machinery, infrastructure, etc. Employment is generated by aggregate effective demand in the economy. Deficiency of aggregate effective demand is a normal feature of capitalist economic system. As a matter of fact, national consumption does not increase in the same proportion as increase in national income. The gap in income and consumption results in unemployment unless it is filled by an increase in investment. In order to create employment, effective demand should be increased by increasing investment.

Consumption along with investment is the determinant of effective demand and the volume of employment in the economy. Propensity to consume is an important determinant of effective demand. It expresses a relationship between total income and total consumption. The hypothetical schedule of propensity to consume in the table 5.1 provides different amounts consumed at different levels of aggregate income. The table assumes total income and total consumption in units of local currency in a society. A total income at 100 units is fully consumed. When the level of total income increases to 500 units, the total consumption is 400 units, leaving a gap of 100 units, and so on. The gap in total income and total consumption is in conformity with Keynes' Psychological Law of Consumption, which states, when aggregate income increases, expenditure on consumption increases by a smaller amount. The gap in aggregate income and aggregate consumption must be filled by equivalent amount of investment to maintain the total income of the society.

Table 5.1: Hypothetical propensity to consume at different levels
of income (units of local currency) in the society.

Total Income	Total Consumption
100	100
200	175
300	240
400	325
500	400
600	475

The propensity to consume remains stable in the short run as
it is determined by the technology as well as by the established
customs and habits of the society.   If employment is to be
generated, there should be inducement of investment in the society.
Investment in the Keynesian sense means addition of real capital
assets, such as construction of new factories, buildings, roads, etc.

Critical views on the theories of employment

The classical theory of employment relates wage rates to the levels
of employment in an economy.   At lower wages, industrialists
will be able to provide employment to more number of people.
Therefore, a reduction in general wage levels will increase
employment in the economy. Lord Keynes criticized the classical
theory on this account by saying that lower wages levels mean
lower consumption levels for masses. This will lower effective
demand and hence lead to lower employment levels.

Moreover, wages are determined by demand and supply of labour in a particular occupation. An occupation providing higher
wages attracts more people. Everybody strives to acquire required
skills to get employed in the highly remunerative occupation. An

example of the occupation of computer software development can be given here to illustrate the view. High wage levels in software development attracted a large number of people to obtain training in this field. Engineers from disciplines such as civil, mechanical, electrical, etc. obtained skills in computer programming to get employed in software development industry.

At the same time, wages cannot be cut below the subsistence level in any of the occupations. Wage rates should be sufficient to fulfil minimum requirement of food, clothing, housing and education for children. In fact, governments fix minimum wages to avoid exploitation of labour in industries requiring minimum or little skills.

Keynesian theory of dependence of employment levels on effective demand has been criticized on an important lacuna. Savings in an economy are re-invested to create new installations for employment. There is always demand for investment because of continuous innovations in the process of production of goods and services. The investment demand is due to competition among entrepreneurs to offer the best possible quality and quantity of goods at minimum cost to consumers to remain in the market and to earn early bird profits. Requirement for investment is met through savings in the economy after expenditure on consumption.

In addition, savings create institutions for management of money such as banks, stock exchanges and other finance compan-ies. These establishments form an industry in itself to provide employment to millions.

If higher propensity to consume results in more effective demand for consumption and therefore higher levels of employment, there should be no unemployment in rich societies like United States of America and the countries of European Union. Population in these rich societies has very high levels of propensity to consume. These countries even borrow from other countries for the purpose of expenditure on consumption. But unemployment is always prevalent in these economies. These nations commonly exhibit 6 to 7 percent unemployment levels, which rises to much more than 10% during phases of recession. This indicates existence of other reasons for less than full levels of employment in an economy.

5.3 Business Cycles

Business cycles or trade cycles are periodical ups (boom) and downs (recession) in economic activities affecting production level, income level, and employment level in a society. It is a very complex economic phenomenon. Economists have not been able to discover any comprehensive explanation of occurrence of business cycles.

Business cycles have become a common feature of an industrialized society. Of late these phenomena of economic ups and downs have started affecting all the nations of the world due to the process of globalization of economic activities.

A standard business cycle is characterized by five phases.

- *Depression:* This is the first stage of a business cycle. It is characterized by a sharp reduction in production, falling profits, low wages, credit squeeze, high rate of business failures and all round pessimism. A decline in production is accompanied by a reduction in volume of employment.

- *Recovery:* During this phase, there is some improvement in economic activity from the lowest point of depression. The industrial production picks up slowly and volume of employment starts to increase. Prices as well as wages rise. The despair of the preceding period is replaced by an atmosphere of some hope.

- *Prosperity:* The stage is characterized by increased production, high investment in basic industries, high prices, high profits, and full employment. There is general feeling of optimism all around.

- *Boom:* In this stage there is rapid expansion of business activities, which results in high prices, high profits and overfull employment. This phase starts with continuous bouts of investment after prosperity in the economy.

- *Recession:* After a boom in the economy, bottlenecks begin to appear in various sectors. Over-optimism of earlier period is replaced by pessimism. Failure of some businesses creates panic among entrepreneurs. Banks begin to withdraw loans from business enterprises. Initiation of unemployment leads to fall in income, consumption, prices and profits. Recession gathers momentum and finally assumes the phase of depression.

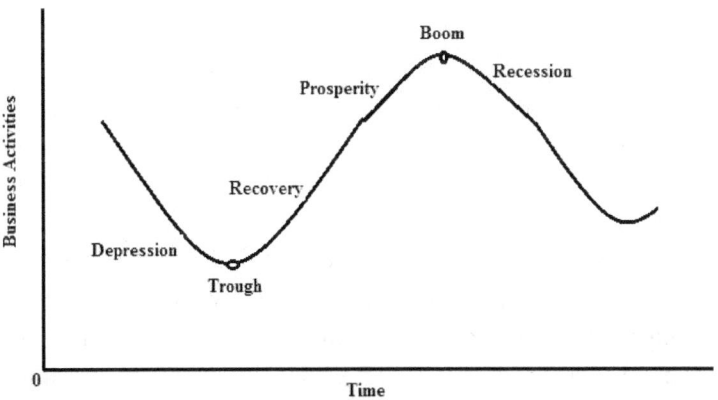

Figure 5.1: Phases of Business Cycles

Figure 5.1 displays the phases of typical business cycles depicting level of business activities against time. Average duration of business cycles is eight to ten years. There are minor cycles of around three years duration within major business cycles. Long waves of business cycles occur every 50 to 60 years as evident from statistical analysis of economic data.

5.3.1 Theories on business cycles

A number of theories have been put forward to explain the process of business cycles in an economy.

Meteorological theory associates the rhythmical fluctuations of business activity with variations in atmosphere of the sun as evidenced in the frequency and magnitude of sunspots. Dark spots on the face of the sun affect agricultural crops, which in turn influence the level of business activity in the economy. The theory is not accepted as it fails to give a valid explanation of the complex phenomenon of business cycles.

Psychological theory attempts to explain the phenomenon of business fluctuations to the waves of optimism and pessimism among business-persons and industrialists. At times, businessmen feel optimistic about the future prospects of business. They make new investments leading to generation of employment and the condition of prosperity in the economy. At other times, businessmen become pessimistic with regard to business prospects. New investments are stopped and existing production capacities are curtailed. This leads to emergence of slump in the economy. The psychological theory does not furnish a comprehensive explanation of the business cycle. It does not explain what causes alternate waves of optimism and pessimism.

Overproduction theory explains business cycles as a result of overproduction in a capitalist economy, which results in fall in prices and profits. Marginal firms start collapsing due to high wages and high prices of raw material. The rate of business failures is accelerated and the entire economy finds itself in the grip of depression. The theory does not provide a comprehensive explanation of business fluctuations. It does not explain why business cycles occur at fairly regular intervals.

Over-saving theory attributes business cycles to inequality of income, which results in savings by rich people and lack of purchasing power with workers. It is also called the under-consumption theory. Too much savings and too little consumption is the cause of depression in business activity. Some socialist economists point out that wages do not rise as fast as commodity prices in the period of cyclical boom. This gives rise to excessive profits, which is invested for further expansion of businesses. It leads to overproduction, fall of prices and business slump. The theory does not explain the complete phenomenon of business cycles.

Innovation theory explains business cycles in terms of innovations in the economic system. Introduction of innovation by leading firms is followed by other firms in herd like imitation, which causes disequilibrium in the economic system. Innovation in a particular industry increases the income of persons engaged in the industry. As a result, consumption of goods produced by other industries increases and there is demand for investment and bank credit. Ultimately, there will be more demand for the products of innovative industry and the firms in old industry will start failing. Greater waves of innovation cause long business cycles and smaller waves of innovation lead to short business cycles. The theory explains all the phases of business cycles. But its assumption of the state of full employment is unrealistic. Also, it assumes that all the innovations are financed through bank credit that leads to inflationary situation.

Over investment theory attributes over-issue of bank credit at artificially low interest rates for the operation of business cycles. The economy remains in equilibrium when market interest rate coincides with the natural rate of interest. When market interest rate is less than natural interest rate, the demand for funds for investment exceeds the available supply of savings, which is filled by expansion of bank credit. The additional bank credit increases the supply of money resulting in inflation or boom. The market interest rate more than natural interest rate will decrease the demand of funds for investment. Bank credit will contract, which will result in deflation or depression. The theory does not furnish a comprehensive explanation of business fluctuations. It does not take into account non-monetary factors, which are equally important for operation of business cycles.

Keynes' theory explains the operation of business cycles due to fluctuation in the volume of investment, which are due to fluctuation in the marginal efficiency of capital. Marginal efficiency of capital depends on the prospective yield and the supply price of capital assets. The volume of private investment depends on the rate of interest and the marginal efficiency of capital. The rate of interest is more or less stable in nature. Hence, marginal efficiency of capital determines the volume of private investment. A rise in the marginal efficiency of capital increases investment and creates income and employment in the economy. It initiates the period of prosperity, which leads to emergence of boom through multiplier effect. A decline in marginal efficiency of capital decreases investment, leads to unemployment, and consequently results in contraction of income. It initiates the period of depression that leads to the emergence of slump. The most important cause of its downturn is marginal propensity to consume, according to which the expenditure on consumption does not increase in proportion to the increased income of the community. This sets a limit to the expansion of output of consumption goods. It reacts upon the marginal efficiency of capital, which tends to move in the downward direction. Keynes' theory explains the turning points of the phases of business cycles well. It assigns the marginal efficiency of capital as the important cause of the downturn. But critics objection is that the marginal efficiency of capital is vague term with several possible meanings.

5.3.2 Revisiting psychological theory

Psychological theory of the phenomenon of business cycles looks the most realistic and promising among various theories.

Psychological theory explains the phenomenon on the basis of changes in psychology of industrialists. Business fluctuations are a result of waves of optimism and pessimism among businessmen and industrialists. At times, they become optimistic about the future prospects of business. They radiate their optimism to make entire business community optimistic. They make new investments in all the branches of economy. At other times, the businessmen become pessimistic with regard to future business prospects. So they stop making new investments. There is general atmosphere of gloom and despair throughout the economy. This leads to beginning of slump or depression in the economy.

A comprehensive explanation of psychological theory of business cycles can be given in the following paragraphs with a new explanation.

At times, a few individuals among rational organizers (including leaders in politics, business, and religion) become over - enthusiastic about a particular type of activity in the society. They present a rosy picture about the prospects of taking up the activity. Results of taking up the activity may be overwhelming in the short run, which makes people believe in the activity. General businesses and individuals start taking part in the activity. Banks start lending credit for the activity as there is continuous increase in profits in the near future. It provides extra opportunities for investment and employment in the economy. As the multiplier effect of the activity starts taking shape, other activities for production of goods and services also show a rising trend. There is overall sense of optimism and boom in the society.

During the period of boom, businesses and general masses enjoy fruits of heightened economic activity. They do not care for further training for themselves and their children with regard to prevalent social and economic laws. A few persons in the society perceive the false heightened economic activities and try to caution on something wrong with the visible boom. But they are termed conservative and enemies of change by over-smart and temporarily successful persons who dominate the society at the moment.

When real issues start appearing after a few years, the over-smart people start failing in their businesses. They try to handle the situation but fail to do so because of the tendency of imaginary things to disappear ultimately. Moreover, they had ignored the training and new ideas at the time of boom, which further aggravates their failures to solve the problems at hand. A state of depression starts and the society starts returning to its natural economic position.

Within a few years, rationality starts prevailing in the society. Failed people start receiving training on realistic economic and social thinking. Society takes its natural course of progress. Income, consumption, savings and investment are at their equilibrium. People adjust their economic behaviour according to the equilibrium state of economy. This starts recovery in the economy at a natural pace of progress.

Many examples can be given for the process due to heightened activities that resulted in boom followed by bust in the history.

Stock market boom of 1920s is a good example that went bust in 1929 lasting more than four years, which is termed as the Great Depression. United States economy from 1921 to 1929 showed steady real growth in terms of the gross national product. The American economy was marked by rapid productivity growth, which was led by unprecedented technological advances in electrification, assembly line production and consumer goods. Americans earned more and spent more on a variety of goods and services. With rise in sales, manufacturers set up new facilities and hired more workers. Millions of Americans began to speculate in stock market in the hope of quick, high profits during early nineteen twenties. Prices of stocks rose to high levels. Many investors made large profits. Much of the money invested in the stock market had been borrowed. Everyone expected the prices of stocks to rise indefinitely. By August 1929, brokers had lent small investors more than two-third of the face value of the stocks they were buying on margins.

In October 1929, a wave of panic swept the investors in the New York Stock Exchange. Stock market crashed, declining by 23 percent in a single day on October 29, 1929. No one was willing to buy the stocks while prices were falling. Hundreds of American banks, factories and business firms went bankrupt. Prices of goods fell to very low levels, but nobody was there to buy them. European foreign trade declined by more than 60 percent over three years. United States economy hit bottom in 1932. Trade went down by 68 percent. Manufacturing was down by 80 percent. Farm prices were down by 44 percent. Stock market was down by 80 percent. Twenty five percent of the work force was unemployed.

The heightened activity of stock market was the sole reason for the great depression. All the innovations of previous decades were still in place. But the depression could not be avoided.

Housing boom of the first decade of 2000 AD revealed sub-prime crisis in United States of America in 2008. Interest rates of banks were kept low for over a decade that tempted people to borrow for consumption and purchase of houses. The Federal Reserve (United States Central Bank) lowered the federal funds rate from 6 to 1 percent in January, 2001. People with poor credit history were allowed to borrow against property mortgages. Banks floated financial instruments which were poorly understood even by bankers. There was all round prosperity and prices of property were rising unabated. The funds rate rose to 5.25 percent by June, 2006. Problems started to appear with failure of people to repay their housing loans. These failures made bankers to acquire mortgaged properties and put it for sale. Soon property prices crashed and there were no takers of houses. Banks started failing and there was the start of depression.

Losses on secularized mortgage assets were so large in the second half of 2007 that they started eating up bank capital. More than 240 billion dollars had been wiped off the market capitalization of the twelve largest banks. As 2008 advanced, the stock market began its volatile and sharp descent from 13000 in April, 2008 to 6500 in February, 2009. American consumers cut back their spending. Large financial corporations failed. Government took over mortgage lending giants Fannie Mae and Freddie Mac as they nearly collapsed with a portfolio of home loans worth 5.5 trillion dollars out of the total at 10 trillion dollars.

Thus, the depression after 2008 is attributed to the housing boom due to artificially cheap credit. Heightened-up housing activity caused all round prosperity in all sectors of economy in the preceding years.

The description of the Great Depression and the Sub-prime crisis have been taken from Desai (2011).

War is also a result of over-enthusiastic kings and politicians who arouse feelings of people by showing dreams of increased power of their nation or society as a result of having control over other societies. Production of weapons, war equipment, clothes and food are artificially increased during war, leading to so-called full employment. At the same time, production of many other goods and services are curtailed, which deteriorates quality of life of people in the garb of enthusiasm of winning a war. The same situation is imposed on the attacked nation. Wartime is a period of boom in terms of production and employment, which has to be followed by a recessive phase. Factories for production of war equipment are closed after the war. People become unemployed due to lack of training in production of other goods and services.

Hitler was appointed the German Chancellor in January 1933 when no other party could form a government. He was granted emergency powers to deal with an alleged communist revolt. He used the situation as a dictator. Hitler promised to restore the glories of his country's past. He called his regime the Third Reich (empire) that would last a thousand years. In 1934, Hjalmar Schacht, the Reich Minister of Economics, started Germany to re-arm without spending Reich-Marks. Instead of paying industry with Marks, bills were raised, which they could trade with each other. Between 1933 and 1939, the total revenue was 62 billion, whereas expenditure exceeded 101 billion Marks, thus creating a huge deficit and national debt. In 1936, military spending in Germany exceeded 10% of the Gross National Product, higher than any other European country at the time. Military investment also exceeded civilian investment from 1936 onwards. The consequence was an extremely rapid decline in unemployment. While more Germans had jobs, a focus on rearmament resulted in rationing in food, clothing, metal and wood for citizens. Rationing eventually extended to use of fuel and production of cars, leaving many Germans unable to drive.

The proportion of military spending in the German economy began growing rapidly after 1942, as the Nazi government was forced to dedicate more and more of the country's economic resources to fight the war. Civilian factories were converted to military use and placed under military administration. From mid-1943 on, Germany switched to a full war economy. By late 1944, almost the entire German economy was dedicated to military production. The result was a dramatic rise in military production, with an increase by two to three times of vital goods like tanks and aircraft. Restaurants and other services were closed to focus the German economy on military needs. Some production was moved underground in an attempt to put it out of reach of Allied bombers.

From late 1944 onwards, Allied bombings began to destroy German factories and cities at a rapid pace, leading to final collapse of the German war economy in 1945. Food became drastically scarce. Synthetic fuel production dropped by 86% in eight months, explosive output was reduced by 42% and the loss of tank output was 35%. The Allied bombing campaign also tied up valuable manpower. In the summer of 1944 between 200,000 and 300,000 men were permanently employed in repairing oil installations and placing oil production underground. (*Source:* Economy of Nazi Germany - Wikipedia, the free encyclopaedia, October, 2015). Thus, the activity of war ultimately pushed the German economy to recession adding to miseries of its people.

5.4 Economic Systems and Employment

Economic systems determine economic relations among humans in a society. Different countries adopt various forms of economic systems. Capitalist and socialist systems are two pure forms of economic systems. Welfare and mixed economies have evolved from amalgamation of capitalist and socialist systems.

Theoretically, each of the economic systems should have full employment, assuming there are no atrocities in the politico-economic establishment. The following subsections take stock of employment levels in countries adopting various economic systems.

Capitalism

Capitalist economic system is characterized by private ownership of means of production. It requires a unique form of economic organization, motivation and operation. At the same time, it requires a unique form of suitable government to control price policy. Factors of production such as land, labour, capital and management are privately-owned. Desire for profit is the driving force for all economic activities under capitalism. There is absence of central planning for investment, production and consumption decisions. Production is conducted as a result of decisions of a number of entrepreneurs. At the same time, numerous consumers influence production of goods and services in the economy.

Pricing mechanism as a result of demand and supply of goods

and services controls all the aspects of economic activity. It guides the consumers what goods they should buy and in what quantities. The capitalist economy relies upon smooth functioning of pricing process in combination with profit motive and competition to produce efficient results in terms of productivity.

There is economic freedom under capitalism. Human beings are free to consume anything they like, which is limited by their income. Free choice of consumption determines the nature of goods and services, which should be produced in the society. Freedom to consume implies freedom to save and invest the earnings.

There are a number of demerits of capitalist system such as inequality of income, over-production, unemployment, monopoly, etc. Still, it is the natural economic system of a civilized human society. Since the start of the civilization, human beings have perfected themselves to produce certain goods and services and obtain remuneration for their work. At the same time, they consume certain goods and services and pay the price for their consumption. People save part of their earnings for their housing, health, marriage, old-age security and difficult times in life. Management of these savings has matured in modern age due to circulation of money and availability of financial institutions such as banks and stock markets. Financial institutions collect savings of individuals and offer credit to businesses for investment.

Demand for goods and services affect their price and subsequently their supply in a capitalist economy. Level of demand for a particular product changes with time and taste of consumers. Despite changes in demand pattern, there is always requirement of certain class of goods and services like food, clothing, housing, education, health, transportation, communication, etc. Therefore, all the members of the society find employment in production of one or other product for consumption in capitalism. Thus, there is always a situation of full employment in a capitalist economy. Intermittently, some persons may be without employment due to change in demand patterns of certain goods and services. A few persons are unemployed due to time required to switch occupations.

This is desired of individuals that they should possess enough savings to maintain their basic requirements for intermittent periods of shift in demand patterns. Saved funds are also required to acquire additional skills to switch occupations to businesses engaged in production of goods and services in demand.

Socialism

Socialism has been defined as the organization of society in which means of production are controlled, and the decision on how and what to produce and on who is to get what are made by public authority. Socialist politico-economic system does not permit individuals to control resources for production of goods and services for profit taking. Instead, there is public ownership of all the means of production. Characteristic features of socialist economic system are economy with a purpose, central planning, collective ownership of resources, equality of income, and a pricing mechanism in place. A socialist system works like a corporate and guaranties employment to each individual in the society.

Corporatisation of the whole economy fails to take care of production and supply of each item required in the society. It is generally pronounced that there is no unemployment in a socialist state. But there is no free choice of occupation as is the case under capitalism. Workers are assigned certain jobs, which they cannot change without the consent of the planning authority. However, it might not be possible to assign all the workers the best suited jobs according to their abilities and choice.

Political leaders suppress desires of people for demand of various goods and services for their partisan gains and for a show of success of the system. There are false reports on levels of production, consumption and employment, which lead to collapse of the socialist economic system. Consequently, crumbles in the economy begin to appear with shortage of essential commodities such as food, clothing, medicine, etc. Socialist authorities allow possession of private businesses to mitigate the situation. This results in re-start of the capitalist economy.

Mixed economy

In a mixed economy, a part of means of production are owned by governments and the rest of the resources are controlled by private entrepreneurs. Overall, governments have control and regulation on production and pricing of goods and services. Private entrepreneurs adjust production and consumption according to government dictates on production and prices.

Historically, capitalism has been in place in all formations of human civilization. Last century has witnessed establishment of some socialist economies. Eventually, these socialist economies converted into mixed economies due to impractical nature of the socialist system, which failed to deliver goods and services according to demand in the society. Likewise, capitalist economies have been converted to mixed economies with public expenditure on welfare schemes on infrastructure building, education and health facilities. Welfare schemes in capitalist economies mitigate poverty and income inequality to some extent.

Welfare schemes affect levels of production of goods and services in a mixed economy. Individuals find employment in the adjusted environment. Many persons are employed in implementation of welfare schemes and regulation of production, consumption and pricing activities. For example, if government implements rationing of some commodities, it provides jobs to people in managing ration depots. Government allowances for unemployment provide jobs to people who identify unemployed persons and distribute the allowances.

Most of the mixed economies have democratic form of government. Democratic systems announce welfare schemes to demonstrate economic justice in the society. Expenditure on these welfare schemes is met through heavy taxation and debt, which modifies production and consumption patterns in the society. However, inherently being a capitalist system, a mixed economy adjusts to shifts in demand and supply due to these modifications. Thus, it should lead to a state of full employment.

But people become accustomed to the welfare schemes funded by public borrowings. Democratic governments cannot do away with freebies, and many-a-times governments collapse under heavy public debt burden.

5.5 Novel Ideas on Employment

As introduced in the section 5.1 of this chapter, ideally there is always a situation of full employment in an economy. The notion of ever existence of full employment could be explained in terms of unlimited human wants and hence overall demand for goods and services. The situation of full employment can be substantiated with the statement 'demand always creates supply'. This is contrary to the Say's Law of markets that states - 'supply always creates its own demand'.

In fact, overall demand for goods and services is unlimited in the society. Every human-being wishes to become king with unlimited wants for goods and services at its command without any delay. This is the reason behind a number of prevalent stories on magical availability of goods and services. People are fond of listening to these stories because they desire too much like the hero of such stories.

The subject of economics is studied due to availability of limited resources in nature and the need to fulfil endless demand of human beings. It boasts of efficient utilization of the scarce resources to maximise utility.

Mahatma Gandhi, the leader of Indian freedom struggle said, there is enough to feed everybody on earth, but it is not sufficient to fulfil greed. Perhaps, he was pointing towards the endless demand of human beings in his statement.

This unlimited overall demand leads to innovations and development of technologies to fulfil the requirements for products with better quality and in more quantity. Innovations due to unlimited demand have taken human-beings from using animals for transport to inventing wheel, boat, ships, cart, chariot, motor car, rail wagon, and air-planes.

Three examples of human requirements - food, transportation, and communication can be discussed here over the history of human civilization to make a case for introduction of new technologies to fulfil the unlimited demand in human society.

Food is an essential requirement of every living organism including humans. In early times, humans used to hunt animals and gather food to fulfil this requirement. They started domestication of plants and animals for production of food. This practice of domestication provided a settled way of human life. With settled life conditions and rules of a civilized society, there have been a number of innovations for production and consumption of food in more quantity as well as with better quality.

Technologies for storage of food started with advent of the civilization. Food used to be stored in the past after drying in the sun, in the form of pickles, jams, etc. Presently, food is stored with various forms of packing. Various types of preservatives are used to lengthen shelf-life of food items.

Agriculture has passed through a number of innovations particularly during last three centuries. Irrigation systems were started for assured production of food crops. Canals and wells were built for the purpose of irrigating crops. Big dams were built to divert water flowing in rivers to man-made canals for irrigation. Selection of plants for developing better varieties in terms of production and quality has been taken in a big way in the modern era. This has resulted in high producing varieties of grains, pulses and fruits. The selection is also made for food with desired quality. Varieties with uniform ripening of fruits and production of seedless fruits are good examples of such improvements.

Selection of animals for breeding for desired traits like milk, meat and wool has been practiced since ancient times. This practice still continues with sophisticated techniques like progeny testing, artificial insemination, cloning and genomic selection.

Recently, there have been innovations like sprinkler and drip irrigation systems that help in growing crops in water-deficient regions. Water-use by crops is regulated with computerised precision farming. Genetically modified crop varieties have been developed to mitigate incidence of insect pests. Molecular biological techniques for selection of better plants and animals are being developed. The new crop varieties are tailored to supply food with desired ingredients of proteins, minerals and vitamins.

As more and more people are finding jobs in industrial and service sectors, mechanization of agriculture has been taken up in a big way. Now it requires a few individuals to farm vast tracts of agricultural land with the help of sophisticated machines for sowing, harvesting and transportation of food grains. Mechanized farming has made it possible to fulfil food requirements by engaging 2-3 percent of the population in agriculture in developed countries.

Traditionally, food has been cooked and served by family members in their homes. Nevertheless, there has been demand for cooked and served food in a number of varieties and tastes. This kind of demand for food has resulted in opening of restaurants in every nook and corner of cities, and along highways. People frequently visit these eateries and enjoy food available in various tastes. Travellers, in particular, require ready-to-eat food. A number of packed foods are available in the market. It just requires one to open the pack for eating food in variety of tastes.

Human population has exploded during past few centuries due to better health facilities, democratic national governments and peaceful settlement of disputes with involvement of international organizations. Innovations for food production have kept pace with increasing demand for food due to the increase in population. There is sufficient food availability over the globe due to the innovations in food production. All these innovations are the result of endless demand for easily available tasty food.

Instinct for travel and requirements of trade in human civilization created demand for transportation of persons and goods. Use of animals such as donkeys, horses, camels for transportation is very old and still being used in tough hilly and desert terrains. Invention of wheel was the result of demand for transportation. Bullock carts and horse carts have been used for transportation since time immemorial. Transportation was revolutionized with invention of internal combustion engine in eighteenth century and start of auto-mobiles subsequently. Today, there are cars, trucks, trains, air-planes to fulfil the demand for transportation. Likewise, boats and ships were invented to transport goods over rivers and sea routes during early part of the human civilization. Today, there are sophisticated motorized boats and ships of large sizes to transport bulk goods in international trade.

The demand for communication is also very old. It started with exchange of messages through messengers before start of written language. Invention and evolution of spoken and written languages might have happened due to demand for communication. There were postal services from all parts of Roman Empire in 100 AD. Modern postal service and telegram have been in place for more than one hundred years. Invention of telephone revolutionized real-time communication. This was followed by communication through email and internet during last decade of twentieth century.

Use of mobile phones is a good example of invention and

supply of goods due to demand for communication. Everybody has a demand of talking to relatives and friends. People used to travel long distances to meet and chat till the recent past. Telephones made it possible to talk from long distances. Still, there was demand for a gadget that could facilitate talk from any place. So, the invention of mobile phones was adopted like hot cakes by masses across the globe.

The above discussion on evolution of some technologies to fulfil demand for certain goods and services demonstrates that the demand for these goods and services was in existence over the course of the human civilization. Innovations led to development of new technologies to fulfil the existing demand. Thus, the existing demand created inventions, development of technologies and subsequent supply of new forms of goods and services.

Supply does not create demand; rather it adjusts itself to the demand, which is unlimited. The unlimited demand for goods and services indicates that each member of the society should be employed in the economy.

The situation of full employment is evident from the fact that there are persons with more than one occupation at the same time. A number of teachers, accountants, doctors and nurses can find part-time job along with their normal duties. Many a times, skills of a professional or an artist are in great demand due to peculiar expertise in performing a task. The demand for its skills is met by employing a few helpers or junior professionals. A well-known lawyer employs a few juniors to help him in meeting demand for his services for court cases from clients. Senior expert doctors engage a few junior doctors to meet the demand for their services from patients. So, there are ample opportunities of getting employment in the society.

Still, the question of existing unemployment in all the nations remains to be answered. If there should always be a situation of full employment in an economy, why some people cannot find employment. Major reason for existence of unemployment can be given as non-adaptation of some people to the rules of a civilized society. And the rule is - one has to get proper training and skills to find employment in production processes of goods and services in demand. The skills also include soft skills of behaviour according to the occupation.

Many persons do not get training in occupations with lot of demand for workers. Some people are well-trained and educated and may not get employment in their domain of training. At the same time, they do not compromise with the nature of jobs in demand, which can provide employment. For example, there are so many persons available for taking up white-collar jobs such as teachers and clerks while it becomes difficult to find persons for menial jobs such as cleaning, sweeping, etc.

The situation of availability of employment in an economy can be explained by providing data on unemployment and migration. Table 5.2 displays the unemployment rate as percentage of labour force, and table 5.3 shows the net migration in some countries selected on the basis of positive net migration. Net migration is the net total of migrants in a year, that is, the total number of immigrants less the total number of emigrants, including both citizens and non-citizens. Malaysia has 3 percent unemployment among the labour force. Still, the country has net migration rate of 1.5 percent of its population. This indicates availability of employment opportunities in the country that unemployed persons cannot grab due to lack of training or lack of the will to take up occupations in demand. Unemployed persons count 6 percent of labour force in Australia; still it can take net migration of more than 3 percent of its population. This is to be noted that the net migration rate is based on the population of a country that includes children and the aged persons who are not part of the labour force.

Some individuals get employment according to their training, but they do not follow rules of performing their duties and are disfavoured by employers. Eventually, they are at the risk of being sacked from their job. With repeated removal from one and the

Table 5.2: Unemployment rate as percent of respective labour force in various countries during 2010-13. Source: World Bank (2015) - World Development Indicators.

Country	Unemployment rate	
	Male (%)	Female (%)
Australia	6	6
France	10	10
Germany	6	5
Malaysia	3	3
Spain	26	27
United States of America	8	7

other job, they become disheartened with the situation that makes them unfit for taking up any job. Thus, they remain unemployed for good part of their life. These unemployed persons have been categorised as irrational followers in the chapter 4.

Ability of people to shift occupations is an important phenomenon to achieve a situation of full employment in an economy.   If an employed person finds that the level of remuneration is much higher in some other occupation, he should be able to get trained in the skills required for the occupation and eventually get employed with better income. This is natural to the law of demand and supply of labour. But many people do not have enough resources and courage to receive the new training, and to shift to the occupation offering better remuneration.

Level of unemployment rises during depression phase in the economy. One of the reasons for unemployment during this phase is lack of confidence among entrepreneurs in businesses. At the same time, job seekers lack courage in receiving training to shift their occupation. There is all around fear of failure in this phase of the business cycle.

The above discussion provides answer to the question of

Table 5.3: Net migration rate in various countries in the year 2012.
Source: World Bank (2015) - World Development Indicators.

Country	Population (thousands)	Net migration (thousands)	Migration rate (% of population)
Australia	23,491	750	3.19
France	66,207	650	0.98
Germany	80,890	550	0.68
Malaysia	29,902	450	1.50
Spain	46,405	600	1.29
United States of America	318,850	5,000	1.57

Note: Net migration is the net total of migrants during the period, that is, the total number of immigrants less the total number of emigrants, including both citizens and non-citizens. Data are five year estimates.

classicist explanation of general wages to achieve full employment in the economy. Wages adjust to the demand for labour in a sector or occupation. There is heightened demand of labour in a particular sector of economy during boom time, which weakens during depression phase. Persons in other occupations start getting trained and shift to occupations with higher demand for labour and hence higher levels of remuneration. But the same skills may not provide employment during the recession phase. One has to shift occupation again to get employed.

The occupation with high remuneration might be the result of a recent innovation making it possible to offer better goods and services in the market. Thus, wages will adjust with this shifting in technology due to the innovation. Also, general wages will rise with innovations and new technologies for production. New technologies result in higher levels of production and consumption that increases gross income of the society. General wage levels rise with increase in gross income of the society as a whole. Whatever is the level of technologies and the subsequent level of wages, there should be a situation of full employment due to endless demand in the human society.

Global human population has increased from 400 million in 1000 AD, 1000 million in 1800 AD, 2525 million in 1950 AD, 4440 million in 1980 AD to 7350 million in 2015 AD (Wikipedia 2016) . Still, there is more than enough to eat, sufficient space, and enough opportunities to work for everybody. This display of data is not to advocate increase in population, but to make a case for the situation of full employment at all the times of the human civilization.

Chapter-6: Existing Solutions

6.1 Background

Human beings evolved to the present form after millions of years of biological evolution and thousands of years of social evolution. They lived like wild animals for thousands of years, hunting and gathering for food, having sex in a natural set-up, fighting for food and sex, and using tools made up of stone and wood. Settled life started with animal rearing and raising of crops for food. The settled life in villages was followed by family life, food storage, tool making, and trading. Slowly, rules were framed for behaviour, economic activities, sex and family life, and interpersonal relations. Over the course of the civilization, human society has faced many natural and man-made problems.

Crime and poverty have been the two basic problems of the civilized society, which started with advent of the human civilization.

Acts labelled 'criminal' were part of human life with start of the civilization. Basic crimes in a civilized society have been snatching of food and belongings, and forcible sexual indulgence. Snatching and theft of gathered and earned food did not induce incentive to work permitted under the rules of a civilised society. Sexual instincts were fulfilled by natural competition where individuals fought for winning a sexual partner. Such a situation did not lead to order in human society after the start of settled life.

Belongingness to sexual partners and children became strong

with settled life after start of animal husbandry and agriculture. Humans had leisure time due to food storage practices that was spent on entertainment such as playing games and painting. The time was also utilised to sit in groups and discuss framing of rules.

There was need for rules for sex and food to bring order in the society that would lead to a civilized human society. These rules were framed by tribal leaders in their societies. In advance stages of the civilization, it culminated to rules for earned belongings such as clothes, house, ornaments, property, stock, and so on.

Rational human beings wanted to bring order in the society about fulfilling requirements of food and sexual desires. An individual was required to gather or to grow or to earn food and other needs. Everybody was required to earn by serving the society by contributing labour in production of goods and services in demand. These earnings could be exchanged to purchase food and other articles being produced in the society. Forcible snatching of items earned by others could not be permitted if a civilized human society was to come into existence.

Human-beings were required to practice sex under the institution of marriage. They had to make themselves eligible for marriage by winning favour of the society and persons of opposite sex by acquiring skills required to earn their livelihood. They were also required to take care of offspring reproduced after marriage. Rules were framed for the role in family life, about taking care for children, about duties towards elderly, about relations with other members of the society, etc.

Some members of the society did not accept rules of earning and consumption of food. Likewise, some members did not accept rules for sex and family life in a civilized society. A number of persons could not earn their livelihood through working under rules of the society and remained devoid of enjoying the fruits of civilization. Behaviour of such people culminated in a human society with the problems of crime and poverty.

These problems are still daunting the advancement of civilized society to perfection. Human-beings have been trying to contain both of these problems since the very beginning of the civilization. A number of possible solutions have been offered and practised to contain these problems. This chapter takes stock of the existing solutions for problems of crime and poverty.

6.2 Solutions for Crime

Two types of solutions were launched to make human-beings abide by rules of the society and bring order on physical requirements of food and sex. These are religious practices and socio-political-economic rules.

6.2.1 Religious practices

Despite framing the basic rules for food and sex, some of the human beings did not act according to the rules of a civilized society. Some people tried to acquire food by unacceptable ways. Others did not follow rules for sex and family life. Therefore, rational organisers (mainly religious leaders) defined religion in the society. They started religious practices to make all the members of the society disciplined. Some of the oldest religious teachings narrate such practices and rules. Human-beings were cautioned on punishment of offenders of rules by Almighty God during life time and after death for the purpose of making people follow rules of civilized society.

Directions about indulging in sex with or without consent of partner are narrated in the books on various religions. There are directions on the various steps such as with whom and at what time one should indulge in sex. Similarly, rules about marriage are described in religious books. These books direct the followers on the points such as with whom to marry and with whom not to marry. There are rules for marriage, divorce, re-marriage, family life after marriage, bringing up of children, arranging marriage of children, etc.

Religions also want people to respect belongings of others, which include earned food, house, land and farm animals. Nobody is permitted to steal food and other articles. Everybody should speak the truth in dealings with others. Human beings should teach all these good rules of society to their children. Religious teachings also tell people how to treat relatives, neighbours and friends on various social occasions. There are clear directions against acts of quarrel, fighting, murder of fellow humans, etc.

Religious books caution human beings about treatment meted out to them after their death in case rules of the civilized society are not followed. The followers (of rules) are sure to receive blessings of the Almighty God. They will lead a peaceful and joyful life on earth. Those who follow and practice desired ways of life will find place in heaven. They will be stationed in beautiful gardens with lot of flowers and ultimate enjoyment in heaven. People disobeying God's directions will be sent to hell with lot of sufferings.

Teachings in various religions have helped human beings to follow a disciplined life in all their dealings. It has made them behave properly in family, neighbourhood, economic dealings and even with enemies.

Even today, religious leaders preach ethics and disciplined life styles. They organize religious gatherings on week-ends and on various occasions where people throng in search of peace of mind.

Technological advances have made people more greedy and restless. They have to work for more and more hours to remain in race to maintain their status in the society. In the process they forget or ignore the rules of a civilized society. Religious leaders remind them the ways of life our predecessors have followed and advise them to act according to the will of the Almighty. Soothing devotional music and songs are played during religious gatherings that induce mental peace among the followers.

Religious leaders preach socially accepted ways of indulging in sex, family life, behaviour in the society, truthfulness and love for humanity. Human beings should be duty-full and have pity on weak and poor fellows in the society. Religion teaches philanthropy and social responsibility. Religious leaders also tell about daily practices of eating healthy food, body stretching and respiratory exercises such as yoga, and self-less ways of earning for healthy and peaceful life. Every religion says that each event takes place according to the will of the Almighty and one should have full faith in Him whatever be the situation.

6.2.2 Politico-Economic laws

There were people in the society who violated rules for sex and food despite religious teachings. Additionally, the civilization with advancement resulted in evolution of many socio-political and economic activities such as trading, taxing, titles on land and ownership of animals. Political leaders defined rules for people in their domain to establish a civilized society. A number of socio-political and economic laws were formulated along with the rules for food and sexual fulfilments.

Social rules included the rules for sexual relations and general behaviour with family members, neighbours and other members of the society. Human-beings were not permitted to indulge in violence with others, cause injury and kill others.

Social and political leaders also formulated rules for undesired sexual behaviour. Forced and unnatural sex was prohibited in a civilized society. Indulgence in sexual acts with certain relatives was not permitted.

Punishments were defined for offenders of the rules of a civilized society, which included fines, jail and even death penalty in a number of societies.

Resources were required to take up common works of benefit to the society as a whole. This included digging of wells for drinking water, canals for irrigation, construction of roads, maintaining defence forces, policing for implementation of socio-political rules, etc. These works required funding. Therefore, rules were formulated for imposing and collection of taxes on earned income, trade and consumption. Obviously, offenders were punishable under law of the land.

In the modern society, the basic rules for food, sex, family life, personal relations, property entitlements, taxes, etc. have matured. There is a police system in place to implement these rules that involves arresting the offenders to undergo trials in courts of law. Judges listen to the cases and decide on punishment according to the prevalent law. Once proved guilty and punishment is pronounced, offenders are sent to jail for specific term of their life. Jails are built and maintained to carry out punishment of culprits. This is expected of offenders to accept and follow rules of the civilized society after completion of punishment. In case they violate rules again, law implementing agencies again nab them and put them to trial and possible punishment in a court of law.

Innovations lead to new technologies for production of goods and services in the society. The new products and services might not be covered under the prevalent law. Governments are required to formulate new laws for production and consumption of newly-introduced products and services. Various regulatory bodies are formed to formulate and oversee implementation of rules for services such as banking, telecommunication, stocks, etc. in the society. For example, the central bank regulates commercial banking in a country.

Many examples can be given about introduction of new products and eventually new laws in the society. Auto-mobiles such as cars and buses were introduced during beginning of the twentieth century. Motor driving acts have been formulated for smooth running of these fast vehicles on city roads and highways. Punishments such as fines, confiscation of driving license and jail term are defined in the act for those who violate driving rules.

Email and Internet have been introduced during last two

decades of twentieth century. A large proportion of population all over the world is making use of these services for communication, e-commerce, and socialization. Ethical and general rules have been formulated for using these facilities on computers, phone devices and other electronic gadgets. Some irrational members of the society started hacking email accounts and websites. Introduction of computer programs that damage machines and data have also been common with special terms like virus, worms, etc. There are instances of infecting computers and networks with viruses, which cause loss of data and trouble to the users. Governments of all the countries have formulated special information technology acts for using these services with provision for punishing offenders of the rules.

Recently, technologies such as genetically modified (GM) seeds have been introduced for cultivation of various crops. It comprises of a crop variety with a few genes transferred from other species including bacteria so as to make it resistant to insect-pests and disease infestation. It provides crop yields without much expenditure on application of pesticides. But it might alter the contents of crop products such as grains, fruits, vegetables and edible oils that may be harmful for human consumption. Governments in a number of countries have formulated rules for field trials, sowing, consumption, import and storage of GM crops.

On-line shopping and money transfer through Internet have been introduced in a big way during the last decade. But some people have found ways of grabbing money by hacking accounts of others. Governments need to amend existing rules of frauds for punishment of culprits of this on-line looting of earnings of others.

6.3 Solutions for Poverty

As human civilization advanced towards a complex religious, social, political and economic society, everybody was required to work for production of goods and services to earn a livelihood. In exchange, it could get the goods and services produced by other members of the society. But some of the human beings were not able to earn their living through acceptable means. These people remained poor in terms of arranging enough food, clothing, and housing for themselves and their children.

Deprivation of many other amenities of life like education for children, health, means of transportation and communication also come under definition of poverty in modern societies, particularly in developed countries. Innovations in science and technology introduce new products for consumption. Our generation is witness to many new products during the last century like electricity, auto-mobiles, mobile phones, Internet, travel packages, etc. A number of people may be earning enough remuneration to purchase food, housing, and clothing. Still, they will be termed as poor in case they cannot purchase some of these products for consumption. So, the problem of poverty started with civilization and became severe with advancement of technology.

A number of solutions have been provided over the course of the human civilization to mitigate the problem of poverty. Some of the prominent existing solutions for poverty are described below.

6.3.1 Begging

Dictionary meaning of 'beg' is to ask for money in streets to make a living. Begging is an act of receiving food and other items required for life through humbly requesting other persons who can earn resources under rules of a civilized society. It has been permitted since ancient times for the members of the society who could not earn their living according to rules of the civilized society. Religious and political leaders support the practice by asking all the resourceful members of the society to make provision of food and clothing out of their earnings for the poor. Rich people as well as the religious institutions have been arranging food and clothing for beggars on special religious and cultural festivals. Beggars have also been provided with food and clothing on the occasion of birth, marriage, victory in war, etc.

In ancient Indian society, even students were allowed to arrange food and clothing through begging in the neighbourhood, as they were not earning their livelihood while spending time in their studies.

Begging is still permitted in all the civilized societies. Beggars throng religious and tourist places to receive a few coins from well-off persons. Thousands of beggars gather at centres of pilgrimage in all the religions. People visiting religious places use the occasions to offer food, clothing and cash to beggars.

Many of the beggars are physically-challenged persons. So, they do not try to find work for earning their livelihood and start begging. A number of normal persons also cannot find work and take to the practice of begging to arrange food and clothing.

Begging solves the problem of poverty to the extent that everybody can get enough food and clothing. But the practice demeans a portion of the population and does not allow them to live with dignity. Persons involved in begging could use their physical and mental abilities for benefit of the society. If they are willing, they could be trained to do certain useful tasks to earn their livelihood. A number of courageous persons with disabilities are working in lucrative occupations. So, the beggars can also find work to earn enough to lead a respectful life.

6.3.2 Alms and donations

Religious organisations took the role of feeding and providing shelter to the poor. Civilized society allowed alms and donations to religious and social organizations to care for poor members of the society. Orphanages were operated to provide shelter to people, particularly children without any patronage in the society. Kings used to donate land for religious places and orphanages.

Various religions preach providing alms to the poor. During

middle ages, the poor were taken care of by the Christian Church. Islam also advocates giving alms to the needy. Hinduism directs its followers to make regular provisions for the poor out of their earnings.

The tradition of donations to help the poor is continuing in modern human society as well. Many educational institutions are managed on donations by rich persons and business organisations. Houses for orphans and widows also receive donations from rich people.

6.3.3 Socialism and Marxism

Industrial revolution in Europe during eighteenth and nineteenth century produced great wealth. Some people became rich while most of the workers remained poor and lived in pathetic conditions. Under the circumstances, some reformers advocated a political and economic system called socialism, which was based on the belief that the means of production should be owned by public and should be operated for welfare of all the people. Utopian socialists thought that people could live at peace with each other if they lived in small cooperative settlements with common means of production and sharing of income.

Karl Marx during mid-eighteenth century came with new ideas with the belief that history changes with change in economic conditions. Each stage of history involved inequality and therefore struggle has continued between those who owned property and those who did not. Marx argued that all the wealth is created by human labour. Under capitalism, labour owns only a small fraction of the wealth it creates. Ultimately, a few capitalists control all the means of production and working class suffers from poverty and unemployment.

Under the circumstances, the working class would unite and seize power by force in a revolution. Working class would have to control the government and the means of production. Finally, people would learn to work cooperatively in farms and factories owned by the government. Over the course of time, there will be no conflicts in the society and the state will wither away. In its last state called communism, there will be a class-less society. Pure communism was an inevitable outcome of human history where each person would contribute according to its abilities and receive according to its requirements.

Socialists started forming political parties influenced by ideas of socialism and communism. Marxists and communists believed that revolution by the working class was necessary to overthrow the capitalist system. Moderate socialists were of the view that educating people about socialism would lead to election of socialist political parties for formation of governments.

Socialism was established in Russia after the revolution led by Lenin in 1917. Stalin converted Russia into a completely controlled economy after 1928. Russia became the first socialist country with a new name, the Union of Soviet Socialist Republics (USSR).

USSR fought The World War II and reached Germany in 1945. The Soviet army occupied Poland, Romania, Bulgaria and Hungary to set up communist governments in these countries. Local communist parties established communist governments in Albania and Yugoslavia. By the year 1947, these nations were controlled by communist dictatorship.

Communists led by Mao Tse-tung established People's Republic of China in 1949 to create a classless society in the country.

Communist nations flourished in the beginning from scratch because of devastation by wars and inherent poverty. But, lastly inherent deficiencies in supplies appeared. Mighty USSR crumbled in early nineties and returned to capitalist economy with a democratically elected government. Other communist countries including China established a form of capitalist economy like those in the rest of the globe while keeping the government of the communist party.

Socialists and communists had predicted a classless society with equal opportunities. It tried to achieve this in the communist world through dictatorship of communist parties. But production and supply of goods and services could not be maintained for long in a cooperative environment where means of production was controlled by the governments.

A popular statement can be made about the fate of socialism and communism: 'a beautiful theory failed by a simple fact'. And the fact is - human requirements are unlimited while Marx said, to each according to its need. Apart from the desire for better quality food, housing, clothing, education, etc., human requirements for leisurely life are also unlimited. At the same time, human beings strive for personal achievements and subsequently a status in the society, which is achieved by acquiring economic, social and political positions. The leadership qualities in rational organisers make them lead the society from the front and cherish their consequent status.

The situation becomes unbearable when human beings compare themselves with people in their surroundings. People in communist countries were deprived of many facilities compared to the citizens of rich capitalist countries of Europe and United States of America. Communist system of government could not fulfil aspirations of people and crumbled to make way for capitalist economy. This was evident from the mass exodus from East Germany to West Germany and the breach of Berlin Wall in 1989 followed by reunification of Germany in 1990.

6.3.4 Gandhian Theory of Trusteeship

Mahatma Gandhi was a great leader of freedom movement in India during 1918 to 1947. He exhibited many ideas on ways of life to improve human society. He put forth certain positive economic ideas based on non-violence and truth. He believed that big fortunes, inherited or earned, did not belong to the person owning it. Rather, the society as a whole was the owner of all that existed on earth. A voluntary abdication of riches could avoid a violent and bloody revolution. Capitalists should realize that the riches with them are the result of labour of other members of the society. Therefore, capital should be used for countrymen rather than for personal comforts. Capitalists should exist as trustees of the property they own. Workers should be paid a major proportion of profits so that they have enough to eat, for housing and for education of their children.

All the property should be held in a trust. Extra wealth should be used for the rest of the society. Poor workers should regard capitalists as their benefactor and should have faith in their intentions. This trusteeship would help considerably in realizing a state of equality in the society. Trusteeship is the idea to bring peace in the society. Industrialist should trust that the labour is working to the best of their capabilities. The labour should trust that the industrialist is providing the facilities and remuneration to the best of its capacities. Thus, there will be industrial peace and the society will prosper.

Trusteeship is a means of transforming capitalist order of society into an egalitarian society. It gives the owning class a chance to reform itself. A limit should be fixed for the maximum income that can be allowed to any person in a society. Under state-regulated trusteeship, an individual will not be free to hold or use wealth for selfish satisfaction or in disregard of interest of the society. The Gandhian theory of trusteeship lays emphasis on decentralization, mutual trust, class duties and ethical considerations.

The theory of trusteeship did not work due to historical chain events of dishonesty and mistrust in the human society. The theory is implementable only if human wants are limited. But human wants are unlimited in terms of power and status. More the control of resources of production, higher the status a person attains in the society. Additionally, desire for sense of achievement makes people to work for raising their status. Therefore, capitalists who are actually rational organisers will invest their capital to organize new businesses for production of goods and services. This can be achieved by employing cheap labour and capital. Now it is for the labour, being rational workers, to acquire skills in demand and get employed in an occupation that provides maximum remuneration.

Alternately, the labour can transform themselves to become rational organisers or businessmen by setting up business activities in competition to the established capitalists. In turn, they can provide better remuneration to the labour employed because of higher demand for the labourers due to increase in the number of business organisations. Thus, instead of a situation of trusteeship, economic rationalism will work in a natural way towards a peaceful and prosperous society.

6.3.5 Welfare state

Historically, kings and governments were supposed to take up common tasks in the society such as digging of canals for irrigation, building of roads for transport, maintaining an army for defence, etc. In a welfare state, the government undertakes responsibility for social welfare of its citizens along with tasks of common interest. It includes taking care of food, education, health facilities for all the needy population.

Even during ancient times, kings and religious leaders took up welfare activities for the people. Ancient Indian economic thinkers advocated a welfare state that was to promote the economic welfare of people with subsidies for development of trade, agriculture, irrigation, mines, etc. During medieval times (500 to 1500 AD), Christian Church took charge of social work such as aid to poor, widows and orphans by establishing hospitals, orphanages and poor-houses.

With the advent of ideas of socialism and Marxism in

nineteenth century, governments in Europe started social security by introducing schemes such as sickness insurance, old-age pension, unemployment allowance, healthcare, etc. After the communist revolution in Russia, many advance countries felt that social justice and reduction of inequalities was required to contain the spread of communist ideas. The Great Depression of early nineteen thirties momentarily shattered faith in capitalism. At the same time, Keynesian economics advocated interference of state by incurring expenditure on welfare schemes so as to restart the pace of economy.

In modern democratic form of governments, it has become essential for political parties to formulate welfare programs before going to elections held at a gap of every three to five years. Each political party lists welfare schemes before the electorate in its manifesto at the time of general elections, which is implemented after formation of the government. Thus, a welfare state has become synonymous to democratic form of government.

Welfare state has different formats in developed and developing countries. Welfare activities in developed western economies provide wide range of social services such as education, health facilities, unemployment benefits, old-age pension, etc. It attempts to provide social security to working class and lower income groups. Every worker is subject to three types of uncertainties - loss of income due to illness, unemployment and old age when he cannot work. The government in a welfare state ensures fixed income to all those citizens who are unable to earn an income to support themselves and their families. Welfare states also provide free medical services as well as free and compulsory education for children.

In poor countries, the prime duty of government is to provide food through rationing to poor population. In developing countries such as India, welfare state manages services for general masses that include medical services, education, nominal old-age pension, rationing, etc. It also executes programs for rural development, labour welfare, development of weaker sections, etc.

The concept of a welfare state is good to reduce poverty and crime in the society. But entitlement to these facilities is preceded by certain requirements of producing the proof of eligibility. It requires furnishing the information in requisite form to claim a share in welfare schemes. Many of the poor people do not possess that much courage to avail these facilities. This is just like the poor people being unable to find employment while it is always available in a society. They just cannot prove their entitlement. Therefore, some greedy persons involved in management of welfare schemes indulge in corrupt practices and eat away the budget meant for welfare of the poor people. This type of corruption is common in developing welfare economies.

Even in the developed countries, some eligible people are not able to avail the welfare facilities. For example, the United States of America has a health care system of Medicaid for the very poor (Eitzen & Zinn 1997). This has been a system in breakdown due to large number of patients. Generally, doctors refuse to treat the poor patients because government pays only a portion of what private insurers pay for their services. So, the poor often delay seeking medical attention. Also, the medical examination is superficial without much careful treatment because the physicians are overwhelmed by the number of patients.

The system of welfare by governments has proved counter-productive, which is revealed during recession phase in the economy. Democratic governments of many countries borrow huge amounts from internal sources as well as from international finance institutions to fund welfare schemes. Ultimately, these governments become overburdened with debt and fail to repay the loan. A number of welfare states such as Greece faced balance of payment problems in their budget during recent recession starting 2008. These countries sought international aid with the condition of reducing public funding of welfare schemes. As a result, a large proportion of population in these countries was unemployed that pushed them towards poverty during recession.

6.3.6 International aid

There was widespread destruction in several countries during the Second World War. In the closing years of the war, an international monetary conference was held in July, 1944 at Breton Woods in United States of America where various countries discussed economic causes of the war. Bretton Woods Plan was prepared to root out economic causes leading to wars. The Plan included establishment of International Monetary Fund (I.M.F.) and setting up of International Bank for Reconstruction and Development (I.B.R.D.), also called the World Bank.

Apart from international economic cooperation, these international institutions promote investment of capital in underdeveloped countries so that the poor countries can develop their economic resources to achieve higher living standards. A number of regional financial institutions have also been started over the course of time. Major objectives of these financial institutions are to help in raising productivity, standards of living and the living conditions of labour in member countries.

International financial institutions like the World Bank and Asian Development Bank provide international soft loans and grants to fund investments in the countries with poor infrastructure. Rich nations advance aid to the poor countries in times of natural calamities such as earthquakes and floods. The aid is regular for various programs such as education and health in poor countries.

Sachs (2005) in the book "The End of Poverty" discusses the role of foreign aid to end poverty on the globe.

Assembled leaders in Millennium Assembly at the United Nations in September, 2000 adopted Millennium Declaration based on the document - *We the Peoples: The Role of the United Nations in the* 21st *Century.* The Declaration sets forth a series of time bound goals to reduce extreme poverty, disease, and deprivation. These goals became the Millennium Development Goals defined as the eight goals listed below that all the 191 United Nations member states unanimously agreed to in 2002 by signing United Nations Millennium Declaration.

1. Eradicate extreme poverty and hunger: halve the proportion of people suffering from hunger between 1990 and 2015.

2. Achieve universal primary education: children everywhere will be able to complete primary schooling by 2015.

3. Promote gender equality and empower women: eliminate gender disparity at all levels of education no later than 2015.

4. Reduce child mortality: reduce the under-five child mortality rate by two third between 1990 and 2015.

5. Improve maternal health: Reduce the maternal mortality ratio by three quarters between 1990 and 2015.

6. Combat HIV / AIDS, malaria and other diseases: halt the diseases by 2015 and begin to reverse the spread.

7. Ensure environmental sustainability: by 2015, halve the proportion of people without sustainable access to safe drinking water and basic sanitation; by 2020 achieve a significant improvement in lives of at least 100 million slum dwellers.

8. Develop a global partnership for development: Develop an open, predictable, non-discriminatory trading and financial system that includes a commitment to good governance, development, and poverty reduction. Address the special needs of the least developed countries, land-locked countries and small island developing states.

These goals are important targets to cut poverty to half by the year 2015, compared with the baseline of 1990. They aim to end extreme poverty by the year 2025. Rich countries have promised to help poor countries to achieve the goals through increased development assistance.

The book by Sachs (2005) describes the path to achieving Millennium Development Goals in 2015 and of ending extreme poverty by the year 2025. The key to reach these goals is to enable poor people to be part of the development. It advocates six major kinds of necessary capital required by the poor.

1. Human Capital: health, nutrition, and skills.

2. Business Capital: machinery, transport.

3. Infrastructure: roads, power, airports, seaports, telecommunication systems.

4. Natural Capital: arable land, healthy soils, biodiversity, environment.

5. Public Institutional Capital: the commercial law, judicial system, government services, division of labour.

6. Knowledge Capital: the scientific and technological know-how.

The poor get trapped in poverty because of very low level of capital per person that falls from generation to generation. Some of the poor nations have the major proportion of population suffering from diseases such as AIDS and Malaria. Overall savings of poor societies are less than the rate of depreciation. Thus, the capital stock declines over time. Moreover, net capital accumulation is not large enough to keep up with population growth.

Ending global poverty by 2025 will require concerted actions by both rich and poor countries. The poor countries must be serious in ending poverty. The rich countries will have to provide much more help.

Middle income countries like China and India are able to meet their need of current costs. Low-income countries in Asia and Africa will require assistance from rich countries to meet basic needs till 2015. A rough guess puts the donors' need to assist around $40 billion for Sub-Saharan Africa, and perhaps $80 billion for the entire developing world. With roughly 1.1 billion people in extreme poverty and each requiring roughly $65 per capita annually, the donors' price tag would be around $72 billion per year until 2015.

The needs after meeting Millennium Development Goals in 2015 would fall quite significantly in many areas. Most of the developing countries will have been freed from the poverty trap into a path of self-sustaining growth. Extreme poverty will have been eliminated from China, and will encompass less than twenty percent of the population in India. In Sub-Saharan Africa, the rate of extreme poverty will have declined from around forty percent of the population to under twenty percent.

The proposals of ending poverty as Millennium Goal are analysed with the following arguments. This is true that extreme poverty will come down with foreign aid due to infrastructure development, and control of diseases like AIDS and Malaria. Infrastructure development will improve general health, transportation, and subsequently agricultural and industrial production. But there are inherent problems in poor societies. Therefore, certain assumptions are made in Sachs (2005) about responsible behaviour from both poor and rich donor countries, which is difficult to achieve in view of the past experiences. The money spent is going down the drain and there is nothing to show despite trillions of dollars spent over the years.

This is told that AIDS programs would fail in Africa because of prejudices among people. Even they do not bother about taking medicines according to the prescription. Above all, corruption and poor governance allows nothing to move. There is absence of democracy or disruption in democratic form of government in poor countries. The dictatorial regimes work to save their governments by spending a major portion of public funds on military organisation.

Governments and bureaucracy in poor countries are mostly corrupt in their dealings of funds and development issues. Bureaucrats indulge in siphoning off funds meant for development for their own gains. Various kinds of favours come in the ways of benefits of development reaching the poor. Political leaders in many poor countries are not sure of their continuance in government and hence they work for short-term gains. Many of the governments are toppled in bloody coups pushing the societies further into fighting and poverty.

Rich countries might not continue assistance to the countries where governments work against their interests. Intermittent recessions in developed world cause discontinuance of aid to the developing world. Recent recession during 2008-13 in developed countries of Europe and United States of America have impacted production and exports from a number of developing countries including China and India. The recession has made them poorer in terms of development of infrastructure. A number of European countries are facing recession with up to 25 percent of unemployment. These countries are seeking aid from European Union. The situation has adversely impacted aid to poor countries.

Populations in poor countries may not be behaving rationally to maintain their health and hence the levels of production. At times, they are caught in military coups, fights, drug addiction, etc. Therefore, this is observed in poor countries that the situation remains unchanged even after huge investments by governments and international agencies.

Despite high levels of industrialization and development on all fronts, rich countries could not remove inequality of income and poverty in their societies. United States of America reports around twenty percent of population below the official poverty line. Although people are out of extreme poverty in developed countries, still there are beggars, homeless and criminals in these countries. Thus, even the rich countries are not able to live in peace and prosperity till now, what to say of poor countries achieving millennium goals with little foreign aid.

Nevertheless, substantial progress has been made as described in United Nations (2015a) - The Millennium Development Goals Report. The achievements of the Millennium Development Goals (MDGs) are listed below as narrated in the report

- Goal 1: Eradicate extreme poverty and hunger.
  Extreme poverty has declined significantly since 1990 when 47% of population in the developing world lived on less than $1.25 a day. The proportion dropped to 14% in the year 2015.
  The number of people living in extreme poverty has fallen from 1.9 billion in 1990 to 836 million in 2015.
  The proportion of undernourished people in the developing regions has fallen from 23.3% in the period 1990 to 1992 to 12.9% in the period 2014 to 2016.

- Goal 2: Achieve universal primary education.
  Net enrolment rate in primary schools in the developing countries has reached 91% in 2015 while it was 83% in 2000.
  The number of out-of-school children of primary school age worldwide has fallen to around 57 million in 2015 from 100 million in 2000.

- Goal 3: Promote gender equality and empower women.
  Developing countries have achieved the target to eliminate gender disparity in primary, secondary and tertiary education.
  Only 74 girls were enrolled in primary school for every 100

boys in South Asia in 1990. The ratio has increased to 103 girls.

- Goal 4: Reduce child mortality.
  Since 1990, the maternal mortality ratio has declined by 45% worldwide.
  In Southern Asia, the maternal mortality ratio declined by 64% between 1990 and 2013. In Sub-Saharan Africa it fell by 49% during the same period.

- Goal 6: Combat HIV/AIDS, malaria and other diseases.
  New HIV infections fell by approximately 40% between 2000 and 2013. It numbered an estimated 3.5 million cases in 2000 and 2.1 million cases in 2013.
  By June 2014, 13.6 million people living with HIV were receiving anti-retroviral therapy (ART) globally, an immense increase from just 800,000 in 2003.
  Global malaria incidence rate has fallen by an estimated 37% and the mortality rate by 58%.
  The tuberculosis mortality rate fell by 45% and the prevalence rate by 41% between 1990 and 2013.

- Goal 7: Ensure environmental sustainability.
  Ozone-depleting substances have been virtually eliminated since 1990. The ozone layer is expected to recover by the middle of this century.
  In Latin America and the Caribbean, coverage of terrestrial protected areas rose from 8.8% to 23.4% during 1990 to 2014.
  Globally 147 countries have met the drinking water target, 95 countries have met the sanitation target and 77 countries have met both the targets.
  Worldwide, the proportion of people practising open defecation has fallen almost by half since 1990.
  The proportion of urban population living in slums in the

developing countries fell from around 39.4% in 2000 to 29.7% in 2014.

- Goal 8: Develop a global partnership for development.
  Official development assistance from developed countries have reached $135.2 billion, the increase by 66 per cent in real terms between 2000 and 2014.
  In 2014, Denmark, Luxembourg, Norway, Sweden and the United Kingdom continued to exceed the United Nations official development assistance target of 0.7 per cent of gross national income.

Furthering Millennium Development Goals, the 2030 Agenda for Sustainable Development has been adopted by the General Assembly on 25 September 2015 (United Nations 2015b). Sustainable Development Goals in the Agenda include the goals to end poverty in all its forms everywhere; to end hunger, achieve food security and improved nutrition and promote sustainable agriculture; to ensure healthy lives and promote well-being for all at all ages.

6.3.7 Basic income

A group of researchers came out with an idea of unconditional basic income to all the citizens irrespective of their age, sex and region. In the autumn of 1983, three young researchers Paul-Marie Boulanger, Phillippe Defeyt and Phillipe Van Parijs attached to Catholic University of Louvain, Belgium set up a working group in order to explore the implications of the idea called "allocation universelle". The first international conference on basic income was held in Louvain-la-Neuve in September, 1986 with sixty invited participants. At the final session of the conference, the association was called 'Basic Income European Network (BIEN)' with the aim to serve as a link between individuals and groups interested in the system of basic income.

Basic income is an income paid to all the members of a civilized society on an individual basis. That is, to each member of the society rather than to each household or to its head. Basic income should be paid in cash rather than provided in kind. A cash form of basic income will not put any restriction on timing of consumption. It should be paid on regular basis, so that purchasing power is provided on regular intervals, such as weekly, monthly or yearly (Parijs 2000).

Basic income should be provided to all the members of a society. Some people advocate the facility of basic income for citizens only. Others view basic income as a general policy to include all legal permanent residents. Children should also be included in the scheme of basic income.

Basic income should be provided without any means test. It should be paid at the same level to the rich and the poor, irrespective of their income levels. It should not be restricted to those who have paid in social security contributions. Guaranteed minimum income schemes in many countries restrict entitlement to those willing to work in some sense. But a basic income should be paid as a matter of right.

During a meeting of the working group in Wien (2011), it was agreed to form a European Citizens Initiative on Unconditional Basic Income. The Initiative (http://basicincome2013.eu/ubi/text-eci-ubi/) has been proposed by citizens of European Union Member States. It started the process of collecting one million signatures from member states to encourage people from every country of the European Union to organize themselves to make a great campaign that will finally convince more people about the importance of the idea of Basic Income.

The Unconditional Basic Income (UBI) does not replace the welfare state. It completes and transforms a state from a compensatory into an emancipatory welfare state. The emancipatory Unconditional Basic Income is defined by the following four criteria (http://basicincome2013.eu/).

1. Universal: Every person of every age, place of residence, profession will receive the income.

2. Individual: Each member of the society has the right to basic income on individual basis.

3. Unconditional: Basic income is a human right without any preconditions.

4. High enough: The amount provided as basic income should provide for a decent standard of living. Thus, the net income should be at the poverty-risk level, which corresponds to 60% of the so-called national median net equivalent income. In countries with low income levels, the median income levels are also low. There, an alternative benchmark such as basket of goods should be used to determine the amount of basic income.

The Unconditional Basic Income is justified as it brings about social freedom, helps citizens to identify with the European Union and ensures their political rights.

Various ways have been suggested on funding of unconditional basic income.

Progressive income tax is the most advocated way of funding of basic income. If everybody has a job with a minimum standard of quality of life, it is reasonable that workers pay a part of their income to finance the institutions. It is also reasonable that those who have the best jobs with higher wages pay more in taxes. This is a case of progressive principle of income tax. Income is taxed beyond minimum wages. Those earning less than minimum wages should be paid an amount of basic income so as to reach the income level of minimum wages.

Based on an estimated household world income of $30 trillion in the year 2000, a world-wide citizen's income of $1000 per year is equivalent to one-fifth of the average purchasing power parity per capita income of the year 2000. The basic income could be financed by net supplementary taxes on personal income ranging from 35% to 43% on the top ten percent of the world's income receivers (Frankman 2008).

In practical terms, financing basic income through a tax over salaries is not realistic, as it implies very high marginal tax rate of 50-55 percent. Also, nowadays the presence of indirect taxes has the same importance as of direct taxes in an organized market conditions.

There is a possibility of funding basic income through a consumption tax (Dreschar 2008). There is a value added tax (VAT), which taxes the whole value creation process. Finally, a buyer will be liable to pay all the taxes out of the value creation process. The value-added tax is the most important form of indirect tax in Europe, Canada, Australia, India and some South American countries. All these taxes may be collected in one consumption tax and put it to the invoice of a buyer. The income out of this tax can be used to pay basic income.

Other ideas on funding basic income involve payment mainly through public ownership of natural resources. Basic income is paid by a government out of its resources. For example, Alaska state of United States pays to all its citizens out of Alaska Permanent Fund that controls its oil revenues. States can be owner of land, commodities or companies, which produce resources largely in demand such as electricity and mineral oil.

A critical view of basic income leads to negative effect on work incentive and labour supply. It might be expected that the degree of disincentive would depend on generosity of the basic income.

Funding of basic income is another problem in implementing such an elegant idea. According to European Citizens' Initiative on Unconditional Income, it should be high enough at a poverty risk level, which equates to 60% of national median income. With crude estimates in a capitalist economy, median income is almost half of the mean household income. The statement is true about most of the countries today. The mean income multiplied by the population size forms the gross national income. The half of the mean household income will calculate to 50% of the national income. Therefore, total payouts towards basic income would calculate to 60% of 50% of the national income. This is equal to 30% of the national income.

Economic studies show that the optimum tax rate for maximum growth in an economy is about 20% of gross domestic product (Scully 2008). A tax rate above the optimum tax rate will adversely affect the economic development. This will further cramp collection of taxes.

Actual tax rates as proportion of gross domestic product for some countries are listed in the table 6.1. Tax revenue of a number of countries is between 10 to 20 percent of gross domestic product (GDP). A few developed countries have the tax revenue higher than 25%. Modern governments are bound to spend a good proportion of budget on defence, education, health and public administration. In no case, it is possible to spare 30% of the gross domestic product for the purpose of providing basic income. Therefore, the idea of providing basic income to all the citizens is not feasible.

Moreover, business activities and employment levels take a dip during recession phase. Therefore, actual rate of tax collection is reduced during recession in the economy. It might not be possible to serve basic income even for rich countries during recession.

6.3.8 Other solutions

There are numerous ideas that guide us to cure the problem of poverty in a civilized society. In fact, everybody will offer a new way of solving the problem.

Corruption in a society creates islands of prosperity with poor surroundings. A few persons in the ruling and business class amass huge wealth through illegal means of avoiding taxes. They control most of the resources for the processes of production of goods and

Table 6.1: Tax Revenue as proportion (%) of Gross Domestic Product (Compulsory transfers to the government for public purposes) in the Year 2012-13. Source: World Bank Databank.

Country	Tax revenue
Australia	21.4
Botswana	27.1
Colombia	13.2
France	22.0
India	10.7
Malaysia	16.1
Norway	27.3
Singapore	14.0
Spain	12.9
United Kingdom	26.9

services. They live a luxurious life while workers suffer due to low wages, unhygienic working conditions and all around chaos in execution of rules of a civilized society. Government budgets remain strained due to poor collection of taxes as per size of the economy. Therefore, many religious and political leaders assign corruption as the root cause of poverty. There have been mass movements in countries like India against prevalent corruption in the society in general and government dealings in particular. But the leaders cannot suggest any road map to cure corruption except framing laws for extreme punishments for corrupt people in the society.

A widely advocated cure to poverty is industrialization and development of the economy. As a common notion, income of the society as a whole goes up due to development, and it trickles down to poor masses and their standard of living is improved. But this path has proved a mirage in the long run for solving the problem of poverty. With development comes the evil of inflation and real wages do not improve over time. Conditions of poor might improve in terms of enough food and clothing, but not in terms of enough housing, education and health facilities. Besides this, income of rich industrialists increases multi-fold in an industrialised society. They use their wealth in planning for production of luxurious products and services. This may include monuments, high rise towers, shopping malls, etc. It consumes resources of the society in a skewed way and in general leads to depression. The discussion should not be considered as against economic growth and development. But it cannot be a cure for elimination of poverty. Rather, the development should be at a natural balanced rate for the sustained benefit of the society at large.

Karelis (2007) in the book 'The Persistence of Poverty' takes account of some behaviours that prolong poverty. He finds five patterns that have been common among the poor and that have played a role in making them poor. These are i) not working much for pay, ii) not getting much education, iii) not saving for a rainy day, iv) abusing school, v) taking risks with law.

The book suggests how to break these patterns among the poor. Freebies such as food and housing should not be distributed as it acts as disincentive for people to work. Higher wages will make leisure less attractive and will make people work. Poor youth attaches less importance to later financial reward as a result of school education. Therefore, low income young people should be offered a significant amount of career-phase specific training. They should be encouraged to participate in post-secondary education. Higher incentives in savings may induce rational poor people to save for their rainy day. Social security payout should be concentrated. Increasing the differential between the income gained from crime and that gained from honest work is likely to be effective to make poor not to take risk with the law.

The book goes beyond a welfare state of solving the problem of poverty by suggesting scientific ways of helping poor to change their behaviour to work, educate themselves, save for difficult time and respect the law. These ways are particularly applicable in a developed nation, as the author exclaims. Moreover, it attributes irrationality as major cause of poverty, due to which the five patterns are common among the poor causing persistence of poverty in the society.

Chapter-7: Universal Maintenance Allowance

7.1 Introduction

Poverty and crime have been the two most persistent man-made problems of human civilization. Both the problems started with framing of rules of civilized society at the beginning of the human civilization. Human beings started search for solutions to these problems as soon as the problems appeared in the society. But the real solution has eluded mankind through ages of civilization, which is evident from aggravation of these problems with advancements in technology.

Various solutions for the problem of crime included religious beliefs and practices started by rational human beings. It controlled the crime to some extent by making humans follow a disciplined way of life. The second solution was framing of civil and political rules of the society, implementation of these rules by policing and courts of justice, and punishing offenders by sending them to jails and imposing other harsh punishments. But the problem still persists in the society.

Various solutions for the problem of poverty have also failed over the course of history. The practice of begging provided minimum requirements of food and clothing to poor members of the society. But this is not an accepted form of living according to norms of earning one's livelihood in a civilized society. Donations by the rich and the governments could not be of much help due to inconsistency in availability at the time of wars and recessions in industrial society. The same has been the fate of international aid. Welfare state has ameliorated the state of poverty to some extent by fulfilling basic requirements of poor people. But it has failed to solve the problem mainly due to prevalent corruption. Further, the poor are required to prove their entitlement to receive the proportion of welfare, which they cannot do because of being irrational in nature.

A number of other solutions like socialism have also met similar fate in solving the problem, which is evident from the failure of socialist governments to produce essential commodities for its people and subsequent collapse of the system. The solution of poverty in the form of unconditional basic income is not feasible due to the requirement of almost thirty percent of the national income for the purpose, which will be detrimental to economic growth.

Universal Maintenance Allowance is one simple solution to the problems of the human civilization. That is, an equal amount of cash allowance to each member of the society should be provided right from birth and until death. The allowance should be sufficient to fulfil minimum food requirement of an individual. It should be in cash currency as all the transactions in modern society are performed in cash. The cash allowance should be given to each person from the new-born to the elderly, across all the sexes - male, female, trans-gender, and persons of all religions. It should be applicable to inhabitants of all the regions in a country.

Any member of the society may face adverse fate due to health issues, natural calamities, internal and external strife, speculative manipulations, economic recession, etc. Such events in life stop income altogether at a given point of time. Therefore, each member of the society should be entitled to the universal maintenance allowance for lifetime.

7.2   Relevance of the Allowance

Each of the human-beings had enough to eat before the start of human civilization. Food was arranged through hunting or gathering from forests. Sexual relations existed in natural form. Everybody had equal opportunity to survive under the natural law of survival of the fittest given by Darwin (see Appendix A).

Slowly, there was beginning of a civilized society and human-beings were bound by certain rules for food and sex. Each person was required to work for production of goods and service permitted in the society. Remuneration received from work could be used to purchase food and other requirements. Over the course of the civilization, some people were not able to follow the rules of the civilized society. Various reasons for violation of rules could be listed as injustice within the society, attacks by other societies that resulted in looting of belongings and forced sex. Therefore, some people took to anti-social activities as revenge, thus further intensifying injustice in the society. Some people still followed rules of the society but could not find employment in the society under the rules. Thus, they could not earn sufficient livelihood to purchase available goods and services and remained poor. In the course of the civilization, rational organisers continued to frame further rules to maintain order in the society. And this is still continuing.

In case every human-being would have been rational through the course of the development of the human civilization, there should have been no existence of poverty and crime in the society over ages. Consequently, human society would not have suffered due to these and many other problems.

Although this has been said by religious leaders time and again that human-beings should respect each other and live life without any greed, still it has not been achieved till now as there did not exist any simple, scientific and structural solution to make people rational over the course of the civilization. The Universal

Maintenance Allowance is such a solution to make everyone feel part of the civilized society.

Starvation is the characteristic of some people not having enough food to eat. It is not the characteristic of there being not sufficient food to eat (Sen 1981). For most part of the world, the increase in food supply has been faster than expansion in population. But this does not indicate that hunger is being eliminated, since it is a function of entitlements and not of food availability as such. Some of the worst famines on earth have taken place with no significant decline in per capita food availability. The entitlement approach directs one to questions dealing with ownership patterns. Starvation is seen as a result of person's inability to establish entitlement to enough food.

Each human-being was entitled to eat enough food before start of the civilization. Everybody should be entitled to get minimum requirement of food after thousands of years of existence of the civilised society when there is so much advancement of technologies. So the minimum amount of the universal maintenance allowance should be equal to the requirement of adequate cash for purchase of food in the market. After being provided with assured minimum food, each person should be responsible to arrange for clothing, housing, health, education for children, savings for old age and all other requirements of life.

This does not mean that all the welfare programs should be stopped immediately after start of the universal maintenance allowance in a society. Welfare should continue till the time each person becomes rational and eventually courageous enough to earn all his requirements in the civilized society. At that stage, human beings will say no to any free-ship. Automatically all the alms, state welfare and international aid will stop as there will be no taker of freebies. When the situation of all-round rationality will prevail, societies will run by natural economic laws of demand and supply.

7.3 Quantum of the Allowance

The amount paid to each person as universal maintenance allowance should be equal to or greater than the bare food requirement. A household (made up of a few individuals) should be able to purchase raw staple food items such as grains or bread, vegetables, fruits and cook it at home. Children should be able to meet their requirement of extra milk and added food with the amount.

Aggregate quantum of Universal Maintenance Allowance in an economy should be less than the national tax receipts minus expenditure of running the government.   Optimum tax revenue is equal to about 20% of gross domestic product (GDP) (Scully 2008). In general 5% of the GDP is spent on welfare measures in an economy. Therefore, aggregate allowance should be less than 5% of the GDP in an economy. Still, it is implied that welfare measures are not stopped immediately after the start of the maintenance allowance. There may be little increase above 20% of GDP in tax exposure in an economy due to the arrangement. Alternately, the amount spent on the allowance can be met from small cuts in expenditure in other heads.

This arrangement of providing universal maintenance allowance looks feasible as seen from the tables 7.1, 7.2 and 7.3 displaying calculation of possible expenditure on minimum staple food requirements in some countries.   The amount of staple food is considered equivalent to about 2100 calories of energy requirement per person per day in these calculations. A part of the money for staple food can be substituted for purchase of vegetables and fruits to make up the balanced diet.

These tables list staple food of majority of the population in a country.   Energy content in calories per gram of food items have been taken from the website http://www.calorieking.com. Quantity of food has been calculated for a person per day so as to provide around 2000 to 2100 calories per day. Daily requirement of energy per person has been converted into the amount of money required for purchase of equivalent staple food by multiplying the quantity of food by the price of the commodity in local currency obtained from Internet resources. Yearly requirement of universal maintenance allowance in millions local currency for a country has been calculated by multiplying the daily amount per person, population of the country in millions and days in a year equal to 365.

Gross domestic product (GDP) of a country in US dollars has been obtained from the World Bank Databank. GDP for a country in local currency has been calculated by multiplying the GDP in US dollar by current exchange rate obtained from the Internet. Universal maintenance allowance as percent of the GDP has been calculated from the annual requirement of the allowance in a country and the GDP. Tax to GDP ratio for a country has been listed from the World Bank Databank.

The crude calculations of universal maintenance allowance indicate requirement of 2 to 4 percent of the GDP for the purpose for most of the countries. Hungary requires 2.05% of the GDP to service universal maintenance allowance for her population. This is quiet feasible as her tax to GDP ratio is 23.2%. India requires 3.05% of the GDP while her tax to GDP ratio is 10%. The country will need to increase tax incidence in the economy to provide budget for the allowance. There is scope of increasing tax incidence in India to an optimum tax to GDP ratio of around 20%.

Some of the poor countries such as Uganda and Ethiopia require higher ratio to pay universal maintenance allowance to their population. Uganda requires 5.55% of the GDP for the arrangement while her tax to GDP ratio is only 13%. Ethiopia requires 8.77% of the GDP to pay universal maintenance allowance while her tax to GDP ratio is 9.4%. These countries may look for alternative ways to meet the amount that includes international aid and public control of natural resources. Apart from tax revenue, government receipts include income from control of natural resources and compulsory transfers such as fines, penalties, fees for public services, etc. These additional receipts can also be utilised for payment of the allowance.

Calculation of the ratio of universal maintenance allowance to GDP of a few countries indicates that most of the countries will be able to service the allowance to the entire population. It may not be possible for some of the poor countries to fund the allowance. Still, there is a possibility to pay maintenance allowance to the entire population in these countries if the amount is restricted to lower energy requirement, say 1200-1500 calories per person per day, in the case of non-availability of other funding resources.

Table 7.1: Expenditure calculation on minimum food requirement equal to around 2100 calories in various countries.

Country	Staple Food	Energy Content	Food Quantity ~2100 cal	Local Currency (Symbol)	Food Price
1	2	3	4	5	
India	Wheat	4 cal/gm	500 gm	Rupee(Rs)	16 Rs/kg
Pakistan	Wheat	4 cal/gm	500 gm	Rupee(Rs)	26 Rs/kg
United Kingdom	Wheat-bread	3 cal/gm	700 gm	Pound(£)	4.5 £/kg
United States of America	Wheat-bread	3 cal/gm	700 gm	Dollar($)	5.0 $/kg
Brazil	Rice	4cal/gm	250 gm	Real(R$)	3 R$/kg
	+Beans	3cal/gm	350 gm		4 R$/kg
Uganda	Maize	4 cal/gm	500 gm	Shilling (UGX)	600 UGX/kg
Thailand	Rice	4 cal/gm	500 gm	Baht(THB)	20 THB/kg
Hungary	Bread	3 cal/gm	700 gm	Forint(Ft)	300 Ft/kg
Jordan	Bread	3 cal/gm	700 gm	Dinar(JoD)	0.5 JoD/kg
Ethiopia	Maize	4 cal/gm	500 gm	Bir(ETB)	5 ETB/kg

cal: calories,   gm: gram,   kg: kilogram.
Prices of food / commodities have been noted from the Internet during 2015.

Table 7.2: Expenditure calculation on minimum food requirement equal to around 2100 calories in various countries (continued).

Country	UMA per person per day	Population (Million)	Gross UMA (Local Currency) (Million)	GDP (US Dollar) (Million)
	6	7	8	9
India	8	1250	3,600,000	1,875,141
Pakistan	13	199	944,255	232,287
United Kingdom	3	64	70,080	2,678,455
United States of America	3.5	318.9	407,395	16,768,100
Brazil	2.5	202	165,892	2,245,673
Uganda	300	37.58	4,115,010	24,703
Thailand	10	67.2	2,435,280	387,252
Hungary	210	9.89	758,605	133,424
Jordan	0.35	6.5	830	33,678
Ethiopia	2.5	94.1	85,866	47,525

UMA: Universal Maintenance Allowance.
Gross UMA (per year).
Population figures are obtained from the Internet during 2015.
GDP: Gross Domestic Product.
GDP figures are obtained from World Bank Data for the year 2013.
US: United States (of America).

Table 7.3: Expenditure calculation on minimum food requirement equal to around 2100 calories in various countries (continued).

Country	Exchange Rate	GDP (Local Currency) (Million)	Gross UMA (% of GDP)	Tax Revenue (% of GDP)
	10	11	12	13
India	63.00	118,133,913	3.05	10.0
Pakistan	101.78	23,642,148	4.03	10.1
United Kingdom	0.647196	1,733,485	4.04	26.9
United States of America	1.00	16,768,100	2.42	10.2
Brazil	2.9753	6,681,551	2.48	15.4
Uganda	3000.00	74,109,751	5.55	13.0
Thailand	33.73	13,062,015	1.86	16.5
Hungary	276.91	36,946,411	2.05	23.2
Jordan	0.7085	23,861	3.48	15.3
Ethiopia	20.58	978,068	8.77	9.4

Exchange rates per US $ have been obtained from the Internet during 2015.
Tax revenue (% of GDP) figures are for the year 2012-13. It refers to compulsory transfers to the central government for public purposes.

Chapter-8: Possible Impact

8.1 Introduction

A simple solution for the problems of human civilization has been suggested in Chapter 7 that comprises of providing Universal Maintenance Allowance to all the members of the society. This is based on the notion of entitlement of minimum requirement of food to every human before advent of the civilized society.

A number of persons in the civilized society are deprived of even sufficient food, which is grave injustice. This injustice prevents the deprived human beings from having faith in the civilized society and following its rules. The arrangement of universal maintenance allowance suggests providing each member of the society a cash allowance equal to food requirement of around 2100 calories per day. Once assured of physiological need of food, other requirements like clothing, housing, education for children, health can be fulfilled through earning by serving other persons in the society.

Universal maintenance allowance will transform the civilized society in a number of ways leading to eradication of the problems of poverty and crime. It will create in each person a sense of loyalty to the society. As the society has taken care of a person since the moment of first breath after birth, each person will abide by rules of the society in the same way as it abides by its mother. So, everybody will become a rational human being, following rules of the society and managing conflicts in a peaceful manner.

Organizers (rational, because irrationality will be non-existent) will frame rules, which are suitable to everybody. Likewise, workers will indulge in only socially-accepted practices of earning livelihood by engaging themselves in permissible occupations, and spending their earnings to fulfil their requirements so as to obtain maximum satisfaction.

Possible impacts of the provision of universal maintenance allowance on various sectors of human life and civilization are described under the following sections.

8.2 Employment and Poverty

It has been discussed in the chapter 5 that ideally there should be cent-percent employment in the society. Each rational member of the society can acquire skills in performing certain tasks for production of goods and services. Rational human-beings help their children acquire proper education, training and skills to take up an occupation. Skilled human-beings find employment in production of goods and services permitted for consumption in the society. These goods and services are produced according to the prevailing demand in the society. Thus, everybody can get employed in the society that provides remuneration required for livelihood expenses.

The universal maintenance allowance will provide major impetus to rationality among human-beings. Therefore, everybody will find employment to earn livelihood and there will be no unemployment and poverty in the society.

Spending income in a rational way to draw maximum satisfaction is also a component of civilized society. Rational persons will understand ways of rational spending of their income on the products and services so as to derive maximum satisfaction. The hard-earned money will not be wasted on consumption of drugs and liquor at the cost of other wants such as food, education and health. Because of all-around rationality, each member of the society will possess sufficient money to pay for fees and other expenditure on education of children.

At various times during the course of the human civilization, there have been changes in technology. There is transition in nature of jobs in demand due to change in production processes under the new technology. One example of shifting occupation in transportation services on invention of auto-mobiles has been described in the section 5.1. A new technology generates much more employment compared to the existing one. But it requires newer skills to find employment in production processes using the new technology. Rational persons are courageous to receive training in using the new technology and get better employment with higher income.

Universal maintenance allowance will provide security and strength to persons who are unemployed due to shift in technology. They will gather courage to get training in using the new technology as the security for food will be guaranteed. The training will help them in getting employment in newer occupations. A coachman should be trained in driving a motor-car and start the new job of a driver. Likewise, a coach-builder should get training in production and repair of motor-car and be employed accordingly. Similar examples can be given for technologies for food production, education, communication, entertainment and all the other spheres of life.

Human beings in the rational society will understand the importance of education and training in getting useful employment. This will become a path to be taken by generations. Thus, everybody will be employed and earning its livelihood to the extent of managing all the needs of life such as food, housing, clothing, education, entertainment, etc. The path to prosperity through rational earning and spending will take almost one generation. In this way, poverty will be eliminated from the human society within one generation after initiation of the arrangement of universal maintenance allowance.

8.3   Income Inequality

Income inequality is the distribution of income across members of the society. In 1979, the richest 1% of American families took in about 9 percent of the total national income while in 2007, the top 1% earned 23.5 percent (Jacobs & Šlaus 2010). Rising levels of inequality result from various causes such as a rising share of capital in total income, rural-urban divide, regional differences, technology change, trade and financial liberalization, privatization, taxation policies, etc.

High levels of inequality are associated with a wide range of social problems. Societies with greater inequality in the distribution of income exhibit higher rates of unemployment, and higher percentage of people receiving income assistance. Societies spend less per person on education and have poor educational performance, a greater proportion of babies born with low birth weight, higher rates of homicide, higher rates of violent crime, a greater proportion of disabled workers, and a higher proportion of the population being inactive.

High levels of inequality are also associated with economic instability. Rising levels of income inequality result in the increasing concentration of wealth, and speculative investments and a contributor to traumatic economic events. Since the rich spend a much smaller proportion of their incomes than other income groups, a rise in income at the top creates fewer jobs and slower growth. In addition, much of their earnings are invested in commodities, stocks and real estate, a stimulus to price bubbles.

Various causes are associated with income inequality. But the main reason behind this situation in societies is prevalent irrationality. Due to this, irrational organisers can find followers in the society and start illegal activities resulting in skewed income and mistrust in the society. Rational workers fail to find employment and remain poor. They fail to impart education and training to their children. There are fewer rational organisers and therefore business entrepreneurs can establish monopolies in production of goods and services to earn higher profits due to little competition, further increasing levels of income inequality.

The arrangement of Universal Maintenance Allowance can cure irrationality in the society. A good number of rational organisers will ensure more entrepreneurs to start business organisations. Monopolies will be non-existent and income inequality will be reduced. A large proportion of population will consist of rational workers who will arrange employment and comfortable levels of income and living. Overall, the society will be prosperous. Income inequality in the society due to availability of fewer irrational workers will be eliminated because irrational organisers will not find companions in their illegal activities. Consequently, a number of social and economic problems due to inequality will be cured.

8.4 Crime

Human-beings indulge in criminal activities because of lack of faith in the environment of social justice. Prevalence of injustice in the society since birth to childhood and young age have created psychopaths in the society. Some of these people turn to heinous crimes such as murder, robbery, rape and financial frauds. The universal maintenance allowance will nurture members of the society since birth and childhood. Each person will have faith in caring attitude of the society, just like having faith in caring motherhood. Rarely a person acts against its mother, as she nourishes the child since birth and takes care of it honestly according to the best of her abilities. Likewise, no person will indulge in acts that are not permitted in the society, because it has been taken care of in the form of maintenance allowance since birth.

In case a person in the category of type-I irrational (irrational organisers) wants to organise a criminal activity, he will not be able to find companions because of prevalent rationality in the society. Almost all the members of the society will be rational and type II irrationals (irrational workers) will be non-existent. Thus, gangs of crime will not be formed to vitiate peaceful environment in the society.

In this way, crime rate will come down drastically with start of universal maintenance allowance. It should take one generation for complete elimination of organised heinous crimes in human society. Petty crimes may continue for a few generations before formation of a crime-less society.

8.5 Corruption

Corruption is the name given to soft criminal acts performed under the garb of civilized human-beings. Many members of the society indulge in corrupt practices while working in various positions and occupations permitted by the civilized society. Some of government and company officials accept bribes for doing undue favour to clients. Students are seen copying in examinations and leaking question papers to get through with marks better than they deserve. Some teachers are also seen helping their students in the corrupt practice of copying. Shop-keepers are seen selling adulterated and below-standard products such as food items and medicines. Business-persons and industrialists are seen hiding income for evading taxes. Medical practitioners are seen ill-treating patients by declaring non-existent diseases, which require costly and long treatments. Lawyers are seen making their clients occupied in avoidable litigation. The list of corrupt practices in the society is endless.

Corruption causes injustice and creates mistrust among members of the society. People lose faith in political, social, business and religious leaders. They start looking for alternatives to the existing social and political system. Ultimately, they gather to form organizations against existing system of government. They take part in demonstrations, which may also lead to revolution. In return, they get new leaders to govern them. Democratic system provides them a chance to change governments in a peaceful manner through voting. But when corruption prevails all around in the society, every arrangement of governance becomes corrupt.

The arrangement of universal maintenance allowance will create rational human-beings who will perform the duties assigned to them with utmost care, honesty and to the satisfaction of fellow members of the society being served. Rational members of the society will own their legitimate income only. This will reduce corruption to a negligible level. Human-beings will live a peaceful life in the civilized society. It should take a few generations after introduction of the allowance to eliminate corruption from the society.

8.6 General Health

Universal maintenance allowance will help in improving general health of human beings in a number of ways.

It will provide necessary nourishment to the new-born babies in poor families. This is well-accepted scientifically that brain development takes place up to six years of age. Malnutrition and under-nutrition at early childhood hampers brain development and hence intelligence levels. Also, physical development in a healthy nutritious environment keeps a child healthy throughout life. Physical as well as mental health at early age will make each person a healthy citizen of the society.

A continuous flow of maintenance allowance will keep every human-being in a buoyant and vibrant mood. This is well-known that more than eighty percent of the human population suffers from psychosomatic symptoms caused by psychological disorders. These disorders develop into a number of diseases such as anxiety disorder, blood pressure, diabetes and so on. Human beings start consuming drugs and liquor due to these disorders, which further deteriorates their health. The buoyant mood of human-beings will help in checking these psychological disorders and general health of people will improve.

Maintenance allowance will make people responsive and responsible to the society. Everybody will take care of others due to inculcation of rational behaviour. Therefore, incidences of quarrels, road accidents, and riots will come down drastically leading to minimum physical injuries to humans. This will result in improved general health.

A number of diseases are caused by poor sanitation conditions around us. A few examples of disease incidence due to un-cleanliness are diarrhoea, malaria, allergies, asthma, etc. Children are particularly vulnerable to some of these diseases. Responsible and responsive citizens will take care of sanitation and hygienic living conditions all around. Therefore, incidence of diseases caused by poor sanitation will come down drastically.

Maintenance allowance will induce good sense to prevail over all the human-beings. They will be cautious of habits such as smoking, tobacco chewing, alcohol consumption, drug abuse, etc. As a result, there will be reduced incidence of diseases such as tuberculosis and cancer. This will create a soothing living environment for families in particular and the society in general. It will also improve general health of people.

8.7   Mental Health and Suicides

Members of the civilized society suffer from psychological illness due to prevalent injustice in the society. Irrational human beings do not allow people to live in peace. They tease others by snatching their belongings. Cases of sexual harassment are more common in an unjust society. A number of persons adjust to injustice in the society and behave like irrational people in their general dealings, which includes telling lies, nepotism, indulging in corruption, etc. For others, this creates a terror-like situation and many people suffer from anxiety, depression and other severe mental illnesses leading to psychiatric troubles.

Universal maintenance allowance will transform general masses into rational human-beings and there will be no place for irrationality in the civilized society. Thus, there will be minimal injustice and little incidence of mental illness in the society.

A number of persons nurture false expectations from themselves and their close relatives, which may include getting good marks in examinations, leading a comfortable life like surrounding relatives, neighbours and friends. When these expectations are not met, they suffer from psychological illness that may lead to suicide. Mental illness and suicides may also be the result of expectation of sexual favours from a particular person. Overall, suicides are the result of failure in attaining a status, getting love and sexual favour in the society.

After successful implementation of universal maintenance allowance, human-beings will understand realities of life as well as of being a member of the civilized society. That is, they are to acquire certain skills to serve other members of the society by getting employment in producing goods and services for consumption. The remuneration received in return is to be used for purchasing goods and services produced by others. In case of change in demand of goods and services due to changes in taste and technology, one has to acquire new skills and courageously shift occupations. At the same time, persons have to acquire skills that are in high demand. These skills might provide better employment opportunities and hence better remuneration. People will not nurture undue expectations in their minds after understanding this factual part of civilized human life. Thus, there will be no tensions, mental illness and suicides in the society.

To receive sexual favour, one needs to acquire skills for getting employment. Also, one has to work for better looks in terms of physical health, hygiene and clothing to get attention of persons of the opposite sex. In case the person whom one loves does not have liking for him or her, a rational human being will understand the situation and will not insist on getting married or having sexual favour from the person. Rather everybody will improve in terms of getting better jobs and working for better looks and displaying desirable behaviour to receive attention of the beloved or somebody else.

Sometimes, the society does not permit sexual relations and marriage with the person whom one likes. A rational person will accept the social rules for sex and marriage, and will not insist on such a relation to the extent of disturbing peace. Thus, nobody will take the extreme step of committing suicide for failure in love.

8.8 General Unrest

Human-beings in the civilized society become restless for many reasons, which may be listed as racism, regionalism, religion, cruelty of police and administrative authorities, lack of effective administration, etc. Many-a-times general unrest leads to riots disturbing peace, damaging hard-earned public facilities, causing injuries and even loss of human life.

Universal maintenance allowance will make human beings rational to the extent that they will not indulge in any activities of unrest. Each person will understand that he or she is part of the society. He has to take up a job to produce some goods or services, which are in demand.

Further, those in police and administration will also be part of the rational human society. They will perform their job of honest implementation of law of the land and there will be no atrocities on their part. This situation will lead to general peace in the society.

In general, those in government and power do favour to the people living in a particular region. This includes spending more public money in the part of a state or county to which they belong. It leads to regional inequalities in terms of infrastructure and public facilities, and creates unrest among people of less favoured regions. The problem is generally solved by dividing regions in a country to smaller and smaller states. Still, the states have some areas, which complain of disfavour. The system of universal maintenance allowance will create rational political class of people who will not indulge in any favour to their region. Thus, there will be no unrest due to regional issues.

Human beings follow various religious faiths. Each religion has its own ways of life, places of worship, religious books and preachers. Sometimes people indulge in disregarding other religions that creates tensions in the society. This leads to unrest and even riots. The rationality due to arrangement of universal maintenance allowance will make people respect religious sentiments of others. Everybody will understand that all the religions have been started to make human beings civilized. No religion preaches against following the rules of the civilised society that might disturb social order. Further, in case of wrong preaching by some religious leaders, people will not follow their lines because of prevalent rationality. Thus, unrest due to religions will come to an end.

8.9 Industrial Unrest

Industrial revolution during eighteenth century led to formation of large firms to produce goods in bulk. Private firms started employing a large number of persons for production of goods and services. Owners and managers of firms did not treat their workers in a just manner. Working conditions in factories were inhumane. Wage rates were kept too meagre to make both ends meet. Children were employed in factories under cruel working conditions.

Workers formed unions with socialist and Marxist ideas demanding better working conditions and shorter working hours. Governments brought legislation to regulate working conditions and working hours in various industries. Since then the industrial working conditions have improved considerably.

Still, working conditions to an extent in the developed world and to a large extent in the developing world are inhumane. Some examples of workers in industries with inhumane conditions are dyestuff industry, coal miners, migrant farm workers, workers in semiconductor industry, etc. Workers in sweatshops are paid less than minimum wages even in developed countries like United States of America, which is violation of prevalent labour laws. In developing countries like India, child labour is still in practice despite enacting laws to stop employing children.

Results of the prevalent working conditions are industrial unrest leading to long strikes, which stops production of crucial products in the supply chain of ultimate products. For example, strike in auto-ancillary units hampers production of auto-mobiles. Strike by coal-miners stops production of thermal electricity and ultimately other industries like textiles and information technology.

This unrest is mainly because of irrational behaviour of factory owners, managers and inspectors employed for the job of inspecting on the part of law enforcing agencies. At the same time, workers in these factories do not have courage to shift to occupations where they might get better working conditions. Alternately, a few factory workers can turn entrepreneurs starting new factory where they can provide better conditions for workers.

Universal maintenance allowance will help in putting industrial unrest to an end by inculcating rationality among human beings. Organizers will demonstrate rationality on their part because there will be few takers of their irrational behaviour in management, government and unions. Still, if an industrialist does not follow law of the land, workers will not prefer to work in its firm as they will have enough courage and resources to shift jobs with little efforts and training.

Prevalent rational social environment will create more number of organizers (entrepreneurs) and there will be a large number of firms in an industry to exhibit a competitive production environment. Thus, monopoly and oligopoly firms will be non-existent and working environment will be up to mark in a pure competitive production. Such a situation will lead to almost nil industrial unrest.

8.10 Unrest Due to Business Cycles

Business cycles are periodical ups (boom) and downs (recession) in economic activities temporarily affecting production, income, and employment levels in a society. Business cycles have become a common feature of the industrialized society. Of late, these economic ups and downs have started affecting all the nations of the world due to globalization. The phenomena of business cycles has been described in the section 5.3.

Business cycles might be caused due to heightened activity promoted by a few over-smart persons. People start believing in the activity initially due to sudden gains on investments. There is a sense of general optimism all around and it leads to boom in the economic activity. The over-smart persons start failing in business activities after a few years when their imaginary projections fail to be realized. A state of depression starts, adversely affecting employment and income in the economy. Slowly people understand the realities of their decisions on income, expenditure, savings and investments. The economy returns to its realistic rate of development. These ideas are narrated in revisited psychological theory on the phenomenon of business cycles in the subsection 5.3.2.

Business cycles lead to general unrest at the time of depression when there is all around gloom with high rates of unemployment. People protest the role of political and business leaders who caused them difficulties during the recessionary phase.

The universal maintenance allowance will make people rational thinkers and they will not be overwhelmed by imaginations of over-smart people in the society. People will be able to make rational decisions about their work, expenditure, savings and investments. Nobody will be able to guide them to the wrong path, which shows dreamlike life in the short run but ultimately causes miseries.

There will be little effect of over-smart people in the society as there will be few takers of their over-enthusiastic ideas. So the business cycles with severe booms and busts will not occur. But humans are ambitious creatures, due to which business cycles will occur with mild booms and shallow depressions. When extreme business cycles will cease to exist, the society will develop at natural and peaceful rate, thus ending this type of unrest.

8.11 Police and Judiciary

Civilized society has been spending huge proportion of resources on policing and judiciary to enforce law and to provide justice in the society. A number of persons are also required for management of jails to keep the law-breakers in closed walls as punishment. Due to prevalent irrationality in the society, there are a large number of cases pending to be heard in courts. Jails house a large number of offenders, which is beyond their capacities.

Universal maintenance allowance will transform most of the members of the society into rational and law abiding human-beings. There will be minimum level of crime. Law-breaking incidences will be too small to create tensions in the society. Unrest and strikes will be non-existent. So there will be minimum requirement of police and judiciary. Expenditure on these essential law enforcement services of human society will come down drastically. Human resources employed in these occupations will be engaged in producing some other useful goods and services for the society.

Police also performs the task of helping general masses by management of crowds during sports events and religious celebrations. It helps in saving people at the time of natural calamities. In this way, police and security agencies will be required to help the society during adverse times rather than being a law enforcing organization.

8.12 Civil Laws and Penal Codes

Irrationality in the society results in prevalence of injustice to humans. It results in deterioration of psychological health and subsequent increase in poverty and crime rate.

Political leaders formulate strong laws to mitigate crime. Many political and religious leaders are seen advocating death sentence in the open, which has been the practice to punish offenders during the medieval period.

A system of strong laws increases sufferings of poor people, as they are not able to hide their small law-breaking acts. Poor people are caught in petty crimes and do not possess resources to defend themselves from the clutches of law-enforcing authorities who behave irrationally in such an unjust environment. They are also not able to fight their legal cases in courts due to high cost of hiring lawyers. Many poor people spend good part of their life in jails in spite of their petty crimes. Injustice is the major reason for non-containment of crime in spite of strong laws such as death sentence for ages. Even Lord Jesus Christ was sentenced to death just for preaching the message of God because of such laws during the Roman Empire at that time.

Universal maintenance allowance will create truly rational political leaders who will understand the problems of human society well. It will result in formulation of soft laws for violation of rules of the society. There will be mild punishments in most of the petty crimes. This will make people rational to the extent that they will not indulge in crime. It will breed rationality in the society, which will substantially curtail incidence of crime. Petty criminals will come forward to accept their crime to face judicial system. People will be ready to embrace punishment in case they have committed a crime. The situation looks like day dreaming, but this is possible in a few generations of existence of the rational society.

8.13   International Peace and Defence Forces

History has been fraught with wars among kings. Whenever a king became little strong in organising armies, neighbouring kings were attacked for control over resources of other societies. Almost all the kings were ambitious to the extent of controlling the entire human civilization over the known world. With improvements in fighting skills and equipments, many nations formed alliances to fight. This culminated into two world wars during the last century bringing huge destruction and loss of millions of human lives.

Human civilization has seen further advancements in fighting skills that includes computer-controlled automatic weapons to attack the enemy installation with precision.   Satellite-linked weapons are used to pin-point the geographical position of the target. Remote controlled drones are used to spy and bomb the armies of opponents.

The arrangement of universal maintenance allowance will help in making the society in a country rational. Still, the countries will be forced to maintain defence forces to ward off external attacks.   When all the neighbouring countries will implement the system of universal maintenance allowance in their society, polity in all the countries will become rational. In the prevailing rational environment, political leaders will not hound for territories of neighbouring countries as have been the history of kings and emperors. Such a situation will bring about international peace on earth. Societies will not be required to spend huge amounts of budget on maintenance of defence forces and weapons of mass destruction.

A   rational   international   environment   will   result   in disappearance of infiltration and smuggling of goods, animals and human-beings across international borders. So, there will not be much requirement for security forces along international borders.

Today, extreme machines such as tanks, submarines, war planes, war ships are used in defence forces. These machines of destruction will not be required for defence purposes when rationality will prevail all over the globe. Rather these will be modified and used in economic activities such as agriculture, mining, management of natural calamities, etc.

8.14 Tribal Populations

Many countries inhabit tribal populations even in the modern age of technological advancement. The tribal depend more on natural resources and environment around them than on the modern means of production and consumption. They rear animals on forest lands, gather food from natural environment, follow traditional customs and methods of law and justice, which are not acceptable in the modern society. They might possess sufficient to eat but their monetary possessions are meagre. Therefore, they cannot mix up with modern societies. Moreover, natural habitats of tribal are dwindling due to deforestation and environmental degradation. So they are not able to sustain their life. Many times tribal populations turn hostile to governments that lead to unrest and even violent fighting.

Universal maintenance allowance will provide necessary cash to tribal populations. They may spend the allowance to purchase their daily needs such as clothing, education for children, etc. Subsequently, they will acquire skills of the modern society and be employed in various occupations in manufacturing and services. Moreover, their habitats will be saved and conserved in a rational social environment without any greed. So they will not look at people in the government as their enemies. In this way, tribal populations will become part of mainstream societies within a few generations after arrangement of the allowance.

8.15   Environment and Climate Change

Industrialisation during the nineteenth century has caused rapid damage to the global environment. The damage has become worse during second half of the twentieth century with industrialisation in countries in the continents other than Europe and North America. High levels of carbon dioxide released from burning of coal, oil and natural gases has raised global temperatures. Smoke in the atmosphere has caused occurrence of acid rain that destroys forests. Pollutants in rivers and seas have poisoned fishes and wildlife.

Global warming is the result of increase in energy consumption consisting of fossil fuels. It releases a number of gases and chemicals into the atmosphere that blocks the natural loss of heat. It creates greenhouse effect leading to a global rise in atmospheric temperatures. Global warming also results from extensive deforestation for development of cities, highways, mines and industries.

Climate changes cause occurrence of extreme floods and draughts. Polar ice has already begun to melt due to rise in temperatures. As a result, the sea levels are expected to rise during the twenty-first century, which is likely to submerge many of the coastal areas.

Ozone layer in the atmosphere is responsible for reducing harmful ultraviolet rays of the sun. It has weakened due to a number of industrial chemicals and refrigerant gases such as chlorofluorocarbons.

Sustainable use of energy is the key to save mankind from environmental degradation and global warming. Rich people use much more energy than required for life while the poor cannot get the minimum levels of energy. Universal maintenance allowance will make all the people to get remunerative employment and everybody will be able to purchase the required amount of energy. At the same time, income of the rich will squeeze and they will not be able to spend hefty wasteful amounts. This will fulfil the energy requirements of mankind in a sustainable manner.

Overall, people will become rational and concerned about the environment. They will understand, accept and follow the common programs to save environment such as tree planting, energy saving, non-polluting and using lesser amounts of chemicals in agriculture.

Chapter-9: Summary

Human beings evolved with the Darwin's theory of survival of the fittest in nature. Humans evolved to the present form about 2 million years earlier and lived like wild animals on earth till 40000 years ago. They had been living like wild animals such as dog, cat, elephant, monkey before beginning of the civilization. Physical needs for food and sex were fulfilled under natural competition among individuals. Strong human beings were able to survive by acquiring food through hunting and snatching from others. At the same time, fit individuals were able to reproduce by partnering for sex in preference over weak individuals. This natural form of life can be called irrational life in terms of a civilized society.

Humans started living in caves around 40 thousand years ago. They started storage of gathered food for difficult part of the year. Domestication of animals and raising of crops for food started around 10 thousand years ago. With the security of food round the year, humans started settled life. They started using tools made of wood, stone and metal. Their interest in painting and art work was possible due to availability of leisure time after beginning of settled life and availability of stored food.

With settlement of humans in groups, it was not possible to progress to modern civilised society under the natural form of life with lot of fighting for food and sex. Therefore, rules to earn food as well as to find favour for sex were framed for members of the group, which started a civilized society. Now, human beings could serve others by engagement in an acceptable occupation and earn remuneration. They could exchange their earnings for goods and services produced by other members of the society. Likewise, they could select a sexual partner according to rules of the society and could reproduce children, leading to formation of the institutions of marriage and family.

Various groups of people started attacking other groups for supremacy over larger tracts of land as well as to gain control over other people. The defeated groups had to part with their gathered food, agricultural land and domesticated animals. Forced sex was also thrust upon the members of defeated groups. These atrocities stopped human societies from marching towards a civilized way of life. Societies had to spend a major portion of their time and resources on preparations for thwarting external attacks.

In the process, certain groups could defeat the other surrounding groups of people. Leaders of winning groups could now command larger tracts of land and thousands of persons, forming their kingdoms ruled by a king. Strong and ambitious kings attacked other kingdoms. They could defeat a number of kings, win their land and belongings, and command over vast tracts of land and people. This created vast empires.

Kingdoms were governed by certain rules on agriculture, tool making, trade, sex and family. Taxes as a part of income were imposed to meet expenditure on common tasks of defence, governance, etc. But irrationality persisted in the civilized society. Some persons did not accept rules of the civilized society to earn their livelihood by serving others in terms of production of goods and services. Rather, they continued snatching earnings of others. Some persons did not follow rules for sex and family, thus creating disorder in the society. This culminated into faithless human society abashed with crime. A few other persons could not find any occupation, mainly because of loss of faith due to prevailing injustice in the cruel society. Therefore, they could not earn their livelihood and remained poor members of the society. Thus, human civilization was inflicted with problems of poverty and crime.

Over the course of the civilization, the problems of poverty and crime could not be contained by social and political rules. Natural calamities and health issues also disturbed the human civilization. Some persons defined religious activities to make members of the society more civilized. Religious rules were defined for occupations, marriage, family and general behaviour with relatives and neighbours. Offenders were bound to face punishment by the Almighty power during their life as well as after death.

Since the start of the civilization, wars among groups and kingdoms have been a permanent activity of human life. Sophisticated weapons and equipment have been developed for the purpose. Automatic weapons were developed after start of industrial revolution during the eighteenth century. A number of countries formed alliances to fight strong countries and other such alliances with the purpose of sharing booty after winning wars. Two world wars have been fought recently during the twentieth century bringing vast destruction and death of millions.

With the start of settled life in the civilised society, humans started various occupations to produce various goods and services. Animal husbandry and agriculture were started to meet the requirement of food. It also fulfilled the need for cloth, draft power and entertainment. Trading was another important occupation that started with availability of surplus food and tools. Various other occupations included politics, religion, communication, transportation, mining, health services, textiles, fighting, dramatics, painting, policing, courts, jails, etc. A number of occupations such as electricity, management, banking, stocks were started after the start of the industrial revolution during eighteenth century. Some recent occupations include software development, biotechnology, bioinformatics, drug designing, genomic studies, etc. Occupations such as retailing, domestic help, hair dressing, shoe making, security services have been in place since the start of the civilization.

Each member of the civilised society is required to receive formal or informal education in any of the permitted occupations. After the training, everybody should find employment in production of permitted goods and services to earn livelihood. The income is to be spent on purchasing goods and services available in the market. As everybody has got abilities to learn and perform certain tasks, there should be cent-percent employment in the civilised society. Levels of income increase with advancement in technology and subsequent introduction of new products. It requires continuous training in learning new technologies so as to shift occupations to earn better remuneration.

Human beings can be categorised on the basis of rationality and organisational capabilities. Rational persons are followers of the rules and Irrationals do not believe in the rules of the society. Rational human beings can be divided into organisers and workers. Rational organisers have the ability to organise performance of various common tasks in the society as leaders in their domain. Political leaders, business leaders and religious leaders are included in this category. Political leaders as tribal chiefs and kings managed common tasks such as irrigation, social tensions, law enforcement, external attacks, etc. In modern democratic societies, they start and manage various political parties to take part in elections and form government. Business leaders start and manage business organisations to produce permitted classes of goods and services. This also includes organisation of internal and external trading activities. Religious leaders define and interpret religious activities in the society. They start and manage religious institutions of worship and faith. Rational organisers are rich class of people as they can decide their remuneration in the society due to their organisational and risk-taking abilities.

Rational workers obtain education and training in performing certain tasks in the production process of permitted goods and services in the society. Subsequently, they find employment in the organisations being managed by rational organisers. This category of persons includes workers of political parties, employees in government and business organisations, and workers in religious institutions. These people understand rational spending of their earnings so as to get maximum satisfaction. They save a part of the income for difficult times and old age. Rational workers are well-to-do members of the society as they can earn their livelihood in a socially-accepted way. They live a peaceful and joyous life.

Irrational persons can also be divided into two categories - irrational organisers and irrational workers. Irrational organisers start and manage production of goods and services, which are not permitted in the society. This includes theft, smuggling of goods to avoid taxes, drug trafficking, brothels to indulge in illegal sexual activities, etc. They are rich people but are hated in the society. They have to remain in hiding most of the time due to their anti-social activities. Law enforcing authorities nab them and put them to court trial and finally they land in jails.

Irrational workers can further be divided into two categories - irrational offenders and irrational followers. Irrational offenders find employment in the illegal organisations started by irrational organisers. They can earn their livelihood for the time being. Ultimately, they are caught by the police for their illegal activities, punished by courts of law and put in jail. So they and their families remain poor for most part of their life. A number of these persons are killed in chase by the law enforcing authorities, which further pushes their families and children into poverty.

Irrational followers are law abiding citizens. They can find employment in some organisations according to law of the land. But they cannot adjust to the rules of society to perform their tasks perfectly. They cannot perceive changes in demand patterns and lack in skills required for production of goods and services in demand. They also indulge in self-damaging activities like consuming liquor and drugs. They cannot spend their earnings in a desired way so as to maximise satisfaction. Occasionally, their undesired behaviour annoy their employers and customers due to which they lose the job. Sometimes, they lose trust in the society due to repeated unemployment. Thus, they remain poor for most part of their life.

Various strategies have been considered and implemented over the course of the civilization to weed out the problems of crime and poverty. The problem of crime has been treated with religious preaching, framing rules for policing, trials in courts of justice and punishment of offenders.

Institution of religion was introduced to discipline human beings in the civilised society. It included articulation of existence of a supernatural power, the God that controlled nature as well as the living beings. Human beings were told to worship God in a specific manner. Religious leaders defined rules for civilised life that included rules of daily routines, occupation, sex and family life. Offenders were liable to be punished by God during their life span as well as after their death. Religions also prohibited existing vices in human beings. Religious practices relieved the followers of tensions arising due to civilised life. Thus, religious practices have been helpful in maintaining health of human beings.

Political leaders framed rules for occupation, sex, family life, taxation, etc. They established organisations like policing and courts to enforce the rules. Offenders of rules were nabbed and produced before the judges. Those found guilty of violating the rules were put in jails for predefined terms for various offences. A number of kings started governance according to rules defined in a religion after the introduction of major religions such as Hinduism, Christianity, Islam, etc.

There have been a number of strategies to solve the problem of poverty over the course of human history. Begging, alms by the rich, collectivism, socialism, international aid, welfare governance were the major solutions proposed to solve the problem of poverty.

Begging by the poor has been permitted since time

immemorial. Various religions preach the followers to offer part of their earnings to the poor and beggars. Thus, poor people were able to arrange food and minimum clothing. But the practice of begging does not make a dignified way of life for humans.

Rich people have been providing alms to institutions started for helping the poor, orphans and other disadvantaged members of society. This alleviates poverty of disadvantaged persons to an extent by fulfilling subsistence needs. But it makes the life of receivers miserable like beggars. Also, most of the poor people are not covered under arrangement of alms by the rich.

The idea of socialism delves to control the means of production by the public authorities. Karl Marx proposed a theory on socialism in the middle of the nineteenth century. He called upon the working class to take over the government and control all the means of production. Each member of the society will work in public establishments according to its abilities and get remuneration according to its needs. Ultimately, the human society will live in a commune with all the people having similar standards of living. Socialist and communist parties started on Marxist ideas could form governments in Russia, China and a number of other countries in Eastern Europe. Most of these governments were run by dictatorship of communist parties. But the socialist economic system failed to fulfil requirements of people and crumbled in 1990s. A few communist regimes such as that in China loosened the strings to move towards capitalist economic system while continuing with communist government.

A system of welfare government is another solution to treat the problem of poverty. Welfare governments provide budget for rationing, education and health of the poor population. But the funds are siphoned off by corrupt officers and politicians. Besides this, the poor are not able to get their pie of public funds in the same way as they are not able to earn their livelihood in a society that is full of employment opportunities.

International aid to poor countries has been conceived as

a solution to the problem of extreme poverty. People in poor countries are poor because of diseases like malaria and AIDS. They lack education and skills due to inadequate school infrastructure. Developed nations help these poor countries by providing aid through the World Bank and the other institutions of United Nations.

Millennium Development Goals were set to reduce poverty by the year 2015. It has improved the situation of hunger, extreme poverty, poor health and education to some extent. But the situation has not improved in a number of countries due to lack of willpower, corruption, internal fighting, etc.

During 1980s, an idea of Unconditional Basic Income to all the citizens of a country was mooted. It called for providing a basic income up to 60% of the median income of a country to all the citizens without any preconditions. The arrangement would help in providing a respectful life for all. But it is not feasible to provide basic income to all the citizens because it would result in very high taxation to the extent of 50 percent of gross domestic product of a country, which will hamper the economic growth.

Despite all these efforts of the civilised society, the problems of crime and poverty could not be solved over the ages and these problems continue to persist in the society.

A solution in the form of Universal Maintenance Allowance has been suggested in the chapter 7. It provides arrangement of a maintenance allowance in cash to all the citizens of a country out of public funds. It is based on the notion of availability of food to each human being before the start of the civilization. Therefore, each person is entitled to bare minimum requirement of food in the civilised society. Each member of the society should receive a cash allowance sufficient to buy the requirement of staple food from birth till death.

A crude calculation of the universal maintenance allowance has been taken up for a few countries on the basis of requirement of staple food equivalent to around 2100 calories for each person.

It calculates to around 3 percent of the gross domestic product (GDP) of a country. The optimal rate of taxation in a country should be equal to around 20 percent of the GDP to maximise economic growth. A number of developed countries already have more than 20 percent tax incidence. Developing countries will have to increase tax rates so as to be able to provide budget for Universal Maintenance Allowance.

The arrangement of Universal Maintenance Allowance does not require governments to stop welfare activities. In general, welfare expenditure of a government is equal to almost 5 percent of the gross domestic product (GDP). Expenditure on the allowance can be met by imposing additional taxation of 3 percent, which is quite feasible. Welfare measures can continue along with the allowance. The arrangement will make each member of the society rational and strong enough to earn its livelihood with dignity. In this way, the society as a whole will be prosperous. People will not expect and accept any free-ship offered in welfare governance. Thus, public expenditure on welfare activities will come down drastically in a few generations time.

Members of the human society behave irrationally due to prevalent injustice in the society. The Universal Maintenance Allowance will take care of food requirement of each human being for lifetime. This caring attitude of the society will inculcate rationality in the society. Each person will be indebted to the society as it has been taken care since birth just like a mother. Therefore, humans will accept the rules of a civilized society as directives from a mother. The situation of all around rationality will cure the problems of crime and poverty for all the time to come. All the religions and the political systems strive for transforming human society into such a rational civilisation.

Possible impacts of the arrangement of universal maintenance allowance on various sectors of human activity can be narrated on the basis of consequent rationality.

It will cure the problem of unemployment and consequently

eradicate poverty. This has been stated in the chapter 5 that each person can work for production of certain goods and services permitted in the society and earn its livelihood. The earned income is to be spent on purchase of goods and services available in the market, thus creating employment for others. Theoretically, there should be cent-percent employment in the society. A rational society should be without unemployment as each person will obtain education and training to perform certain useful task in the society. Each employed person will be able to sustain livelihood for self and its family. In this way, poverty will be eradicated from the human society. The problem of income inequality will be solved due to full employment bringing about all around prosperity in the society.

A rational social environment will have positive effect on general health of people. Members of the society will take care of sanitation around them. They will stop fighting every now and then, thus saving themselves from injuries. There will be fewer road accidents due to obedient drivers. These situations will improve general health of people. A just social environment will improve mental health also. Infants and children will get sufficient nutritious food and will not be mentally retarded due to nutrient deficiencies during early childhood.

Irrational organisers will be non-existent in the society. In case somebody tries to organise illegal activities, it will not be possible in the absence of irrational workers. Thus, the society will be without organised crime. Petty criminals will be few and without any support due to all around rationality. Public expenditure on police, judiciary and jails will be reduced drastically in the near absence of crime.

Many a times there is general unrest in the society due to regionalism, religion and other acts of favouritism by rational organisers to their relatives and friends. Likewise, industrial unrest due to inhumane working conditions and low wages have become quite common after start of the industrial revolution during the eighteenth century. Unrest during recessionary phase of business cycles also disturb peace in the society.

Rational organisers will not favour any region and religion after start of universal maintenance allowance. It will be quite impossible to engage persons in industries with inhumane conditions. Rational workers will have enough courage to shift occupations after receiving appropriate training to earn better remuneration in an humane environment. So, they will not start industrial strikes with demands on working conditions and better wages. Likewise, they will not rush after heightened activities started by rational organisers and severe phases of business cycles will not occur in the economy. Thus, all these types of unrest will cease to exist in the society leading to a peaceful human civilization.

The arrangement of universal maintenance allowance will improve international relations after its implementation across borders. Population as well as leaders of neighbouring countries will not think of violating borders and international treaties. Thus, there will be peace on international borders. It will reduce the expenditure on defence forces and public money will be used on infrastructure building and social welfare. Police and security forces will be mainly required to mitigate natural calamities and for management of people during social gatherings and sports.

A good portion of human population is still not part of the civilised society to the full extent. This includes tribal population living in forests and remote hilly areas. Universal maintenance allowance will put them on the main social stream due to availability of required cash in their hands. These neglected people will consider themselves part of the society while living in their habitats. They will engage themselves in useful activities due to rational behaviour of all the persons. Thus, they will become part of the mainstream and modern human civilization.

The arrangement of Universal Maintenance Allowance since birth to every person in the society will start a rational human civilisation where each member of the society will obey rules of the society. Conflicts amongst persons, organisations and nations will be resolved through discussions and there will be all around peace on earth. Each member will be able to find employment to earn sufficient remuneration to spend the earnings on food, housing, clothing, education, health and other goods and services available in the market as rational economic individual. Thus, human civilization in every nook and corner of the earth will be prosperous in spite of continuance of income inequalities. When each person will live in peace, and will be able to purchase each of the goods and services available in the market, this will create a situation of parity in the human society. Overall there will be peace, parity and prosperity on the globe.

Appendix-A: Natural and Economics Terminology

Aggregate Effective Demand: Aggregate effective demand comprises of the expenditure on consumption goods as well as on investment goods in an economy. Keynesian General Theory is an analysis of aggregate effective demand, which depends on propensity to consume and inducement to invest. A third determinant of effective demand is government expenditure on consumption and investment goods.

Darwin's Theory of Evolution: Charles Darwin published the book *On the Origin of Species* in 1859 after studying plant and animal life for 25 years. It presented a theory of evolution on how new types of organisms develop in nature. The theory explains how species evolve through natural selection.

Organisms produce several offspring, each possessing a unique set of characteristics. Some individuals have the characteristics that enable them to obtain food, mates for sex, territory and disease resistance. These individuals survive, reproduce and pass on their characteristics to their offspring. Weak individuals die before they reproduce, and their unsuitable characteristics appear less frequently in a population. Thus, there is natural selection of individuals best suited in an environment.

Environment is always changing in terms of temperature and precipitation. Some species are able to adapt to the new environmental conditions. Small changes through mutation always occur in the set of characteristics of individuals. Parents pass along useful characteristics to their offspring through the process of evolution. With enough small changes over a long period of time, the survivors become different from their ancestors, thus evolving new species.

Deoxyribo-Nucleic Acid (DNA): is the genetic material in all the organisms from viruses, bacteria, plants and animals. It is made up of four bases: adenine (A), guanine (G), cytosine (C), and thymine (T). The sequence of these bases determines synthesis of proteins for building and shaping organisms.

Developed Countries: A developed country is a sovereign state that has a highly developed economy and advanced technological infrastructure relative to other less industrialised nations. Most commonly, the criteria for evaluating the degree of economic development are gross domestic product (GDP), per capita income, level of industrialization, amount of widespread infrastructure and general standards of living.

Economies of Scale: These refer to the savings as a result of reduction in average production cost due to increase in size of production unit. Increase in plant size reduces the average cost of production. Internal economies of scale result from increased size of an individual firm while external economies result from increased size of the industry. Internal economies are the result of mass production and due to advantage of specialization in production of a particular class of goods and services.

Evolution: Evolution generally refers to the process of change over time in life forms.

Fertile Crescent: It is the region beginning from the eastern end of the Mediterranean Sea and passing through south of Asia Minor and Armenia where it curves southwards towards the valley of Tigris and Euphrates rivers. Parts of land in this region are fertile. Early human civilizations developed and flourished in this region.

Feudalism: This is a political system based on small, local power centres working as government.

Gini Coefficient: Gini coefficient is a measure to quantify inequality in income and wealth in a society. It is defined with the following formula.

$$\frac{1}{2n^2\bar{x}} \sum_{i=1}^{n} \sum_{j=1}^{n} |x_i - x_j|$$

where $\bar{x} = \frac{1}{n} \sum_{i=1}^{n} x_i$ denotes mean income. Gini coefficient is average of absolute differences between all possible pairs (i, j) of income receivers in a society (Cowell 2007).

Globalization: Globalization is the process of international integration arising from the interchange of world views, products, ideas and other aspects of culture with advances in transportation and telecommunication.

Gross Domestic Product (GDP): GDP of a country is aggregate value of all the goods and services produced in the country in a period. It is generally measured on yearly basis.

Imperialism: is the practice of empire building by establishing colonies in order to control raw materials and markets.

Marginal Efficiency of Capital (MEC): MEC is the highest rate of return over cost accruing from an additional unit of investment. The essential condition for fresh investment in an economy is that the MEC of a new capital asset should be considerably in access of the market rate of interest.

Medieval Period: Also called middle ages, the period after collapse of the Roman Empire till the modern age is considered the medieval period. It is generally marked from 500 to 1500 AD. Feudalism was the hallmark of middle ages.

Monopoly: Monopoly is a market structure where only one seller exists for a particular product or service. The situation arises where the optimum scale for the product is so large that there is room for only one producer, for example, electric power. In some cases, the seller is able to prevent entry of new producers in the market because of holding of patent for the product. Anyone who tries to duplicate the product is liable to suit for infringement of the patent.

Monopolistic Competition: In this type of market structure, there are a number of sellers and buyers of the differentiated form of a product. Various products of sellers are not considered perfect substitutes by buyers. Thus, each producer has a limited monopoly of its own product.

Multiplier Effect: Multiplier effect is the ratio of change in income to the change in investment in an economy. It explains how many times the effect of an initial change in investment is multiplied by causing change in consumption and finally in aggregate income. Original investment increases income not only in the industries where the investment is made, but also in other industries due to increase in income and subsequent demand. Thus, there is a multiple order of increase in income in the economy over an increase in the amount of investment.

Mercantilism: The term applies to those theories, policies and practices arising from conditions of time, by which the state sought to increase its own power, wealth and prosperity. Mercantilism helped the European countries in adopting a national commercial policy during the period of colonialism.

Poverty line: Poverty line is an absolute level of income, which will enable a family to live at some minimal level. A basket of modest array of food, clothing, rent, etc. is priced to find out what this will cost over a year's time. Families not having enough income to achieve a minimal standard of living are below poverty line. Rich and poor countries have different living standards, and hence differ in poverty line. Poverty line also varies with time in the same country as standards of living change over time.

Principle of Diminishing Marginal Utility: Marginal utility corresponds to the satisfaction derived from the additional unit of goods or services consumed in a specific time period. The principle of diminishing marginal utility states that the additional satisfaction (utility) derived from consumption of each additional unit of an item decreases continuously. It leads to a simple rule of spending money on purchasing items so as to achieve the greatest satisfaction out of additional spending.

Propensity to Consume: This is the proportion of income, which is consumed in an economy. The schedule of propensity to consume expresses a relationship between total income and total consumption. It is derived from Keynes' psychological law of consumption, which states that the consumption expenditure increases by a smaller amount with increase in income.

Purchasing Power Parity (PPP): The concept of purchasing power parity allows one to estimate the exchange rate between two currencies for it to be at par with the purchasing power of the two countries' currencies. PPP rates help to minimize misleading international comparisons that can arise with the use of market exchange rates.

Psychopaths: are humans with personality disorders characterised by unsocial and impulsive behaviour.

Pure Competition: This represents a market structure with many sellers and buyers of a homogeneous product. There is no entry barrier to market and nobody can fix the prices. Price for a product depends solely on the level of its demand.

Renaissance: There were changes in human attitude that grew out of philosophical and artistic movement in Europe during medieval times during 1350-1700 AD. This movement known as renaissance, a French word meaning rebirth, centered on revival of interest in the classical learnings of Greece and Rome. The period of renaissance saw many important developments such as invention of the printing press, and advances in science with emphasis on reasoning.

Republic: A republic is a form of government where those entitled to vote choose the people to run the government.

Substitution Effect: If two or more products can satisfy a particular want, consumers can buy either of the products according to their price to draw desired satisfaction. Thus, the demand for a product depends on price levels of other substituting products. Substitution effect influences decision of an individual to buy less of any goods and services, which has risen in price relative to other items of consumption.

Underdeveloped Country: An underdeveloped country is characterised by the co-existence of un-utilised or under-utilised man-power as well as of unexplored natural resources on account of low rate of capital formation. Per-capita income is extremely low in the economy. There is chronic deficiency of capital as well. People are mainly dependent on primary occupations such as agriculture and mining, employing primitive technology.

Appendix-B: Personality Disorders

Human beings in general develop customary and comfortable patterns of handling situations within their social environment. They have the capability to make decisions according to the situation and adjust themselves for fruitful life. But in individuals diagnosed to be suffering from a personality disorder, these patterns show rigidity, which makes them counter-adaptive. These persons are not bothered by their troubling behaviour, even though it may concern friends and relatives. Personality disorders provide a framework to determine when persons are functioning well or poorly.

A few well-characterized personality disorders are listed below (Nathan & Harris 1980).

Paranoid Personality Disorder: These people are likely to be extremely sensitive to other people's behaviour and to interpret it in suspicious light. They blame others for their shortcomings and failures and, as a result, usually have few friends.

Schizoid Personality Disorder: These people tend to be withdrawn and reclusive. They avoid close inter-personal relationships and make their emotional investments more often in ideas than in people.

Compulsive Personality Disorders: These people aim to attain perfection and orderliness in everything they do. They are inhibited in their expression of feelings, meticulous in their behaviour, excessively diligent and duty-bound in their execution of responsibilities. They are unable to relax. Compulsive personality may be adaptive for a person who is in an occupation requiring considerable attention to detail and concentration on a repetitive task. The same high standards may make it difficult for them to find people whom they regard adequate.

Histrionic Personality Disorder: Histrionic personality exhibits a pattern of behaviour marked by excitability, self-centeredness, rapidly shifting but shallow effect, and over-reactivity. These people may strive to be the focus of attention through dramatic, often striking behaviour.

Passive-Aggressive Personality Disorder: People with this disorder display both passivity, and aggressiveness and hostility. The aggressive aspect of their behaviour may be expressed in a positive mode as disguised hostility. Unable to express aggression directly, these persons structure life to stay wide-eyed and innocent. The line between normal controlled anger and positive-aggressive personality is difficult to draw.

Schizotypal Personality Disorder: It includes people with incapacity to develop social relationships, introversion and circumscribed mood. They have few or no close friends, appear not to need or desire them, seem to be unresponsive to the effects of either praise or blame, and appear to be insensitive to the needs of others. They seem to be without humour or hostility.

Borderline Personality Disorder: It is characterised by distortions in inter-personal relationships, behaviour, mood, and self-perception. There is frequent shifting of problematic behaviour. Their eccentricities, self-centeredness, tendency to over-indulge and to under control behaviour, and inability or unwillingness to stabilise moods - all contribute to the widespread conviction that they cannot relate either to groups or to individuals.

Avoidant Personality Disorder: Hallmarks of the disorder are extreme sensitivity to the slightest hint of emotional or intellectual rejection, unwillingness to initiate inter-personal relationships without absolute assurance that they will result in unquestioning acceptance, low self-esteem and little sense of self-worth. These people often find themselves alone even though they want and need others.

Dependent Personality Disorder: There is a continuing quest for someone who will assume responsibility for one's life and decisions. These persons have total lack of self-esteem combined with intense unhappiness on having to be alone for even brief periods of time.

Narcissistic Personality Disorder: People with this disorder have an exaggerated sense of self-importance, achievements, and potential. They are often preoccupied with fantasies of their own strength, power, attractiveness, and brilliance. They find it difficult to respond objectively to criticism, and cannot empathise with others' problems.

Antisocial Personality Disorder: Antisocial person is selfish, impulsive, unable to learn from experience, and cannot tolerate frustration or cope with demands to delay reinforcement. Such individuals want to fulfil their desires at any cost.

Bibliography

Banerjee, Abhijit V., & Duflo, Esther. 2011. *Poor Economics.* Random House India, Noida.

Barraclough, Geoffrey, & Overy, Richard (eds). 2009. *Complete History of the World.* HarperCollins Publishers, India.
Some contents on history of the World have been taken from this book.

Beattie, Alan. 2009. *False Economy: A Surprising Economic History of the World.* Penguin Books, London.

Buss, David M. 2008. *Evolutionary Psychology: The New Science of the Mind.* Third edn. Pearson Education, Inc. Indian edition: Dorling Kindersley India Pvt. Ltd. 2009.

Calorieking. 2015. *Calories in food.* http://www.calorieking.com.
Calorific values of various staple foods have been noted from this website.

Cowell, Frank A. 2007. *Income Distribution and Inequality.* DARP 94, STICERD, London School of Economics.

Davis, M. Dale. 1994. *Civilizations in History.* Second edn. Oxford University Press, Toronto.
Description of Darwin's Theory of Evolution has been taken from the book. Some of the early history of civilisation has also been taken from this book.

Desai, Padma. 2011. *From Financial Crisis to Global Recovery*. Columbia University Press; Indian edition, 2012: Collins Business - An imprint of HarperCollins Publishers India.

Dreschar, Jőrg. 2008. *Economic view of model proposals for funding a basic income on the basis of the value creation of goods and services*. http://www.jovialis.org.

Eitzen, D. Stanley, & Zinn, Maxine Baca. 1997. *Social Problems*. Seventh edn. Allyn and Bacon, MA.

Frankman, Myron J. 2008. *Justice, sustainability and progressive taxation and redistribution: the case for a world-wide basic income*. 12th Biennial Meeting of Basic Income Earth Network (BIEN), Dublin, Ireland, June 20-21, 2008.

Gentilini, Ugo, & Sumner, Andy. 2012. *What Do National Poverty Lines Tell Us About Global Poverty?* Tech. rept. IDS Working Paper 392. Institute of Development Studies, Brighton BN1 9RE, UK.

Jacobs, Garry, & Šlaus, Ivo. 2010. Indicators of economics progress: the power of measurement and human welfare. *Cadmus*, **1**(1), 53–113.

Karelis, Charles. 2007. *The Persistence of Poverty - Why the Economics of the Well-off Can't Help the Poor*. Yale University Press; Oxford University Press, New Delhi, 2012.

Madrigal, Francisco Javier Alonso, & Perez, Jose Luis Rey. 2007. *What type of taxes demand basic income?*

Majumdar, R. C., Raychaudhuri, H. C., & Datta, K. 1978. *An Advanced History of India*. Fourth edn. Macmillan India Limited.
A few events in Indian history have been taken from this book.

Mazour, Anatole G., Peoples, John M., & Rabb, Theoddore K. 1987. *People and Nations - A World History*. Harcourt Brace Jovanovich, Orlando.
Most of the historical rumblings in various chapters have been taken from this book. It is main source of the contents of the chapter on brief history of civilization. The contents on evolution of various occupations are also taken from the book.

Nathan, Peter E., & Harris, Sandra L. 1980. *Psychopathology and Society*. Second edn. McGraw Book Company, New York.

OECD. 2011. Equity Indicators. *Chap. 6 of: Society at a Glance: OECD Social Indicators*. OECD Publishing.

Parijs, Philippe Van. 2000. Basic income: a simple and powerful idea for 21st century. *In: Basic Income European Network VIIIth International Congress, Berlin*.

Rees, Linford. 1982. *A Short Textbook of Psychiatry*. Third edn. The English Language Book Society (ELBS), Hodder and Stoughton.

Reynolds, Lloyd G. 1979. *Microeconomics*. Third edn. Richard D. Irwin Inc. Illinois.
Definitions of a few economics terminologies are noted from this book.

Sachs, Jeffrey D. 2005. *The End of Poverty - How We Can Make It Happen in Our Lifetime*. Penguin Books, London.

Scully, Gerald W. 2008. *Optimal Taxation, Economic Growth and Income Inequality in the United States*. Tech. rept. 316. National Center for Policy Analysis, Dallas, TX.

Sen, Amartya. 1981. *Poverty and Famines - An Essay on Entitlement and Deprivation*. Oxford University Press, New York; Oxford India Paperbacks, New Delhi, 1999.

Seth, M. L. 1988. *Macroeconomics*. Tenth edn. Lakshmi Narain Agarwal Educational Publishers, Agra, India.
Most of the contents on economic concepts have been taken from this book. It is also the source of theories on employment and business cycles.

Singh, Bhagwan. 2004. *Bhartiya Sabhyata Kee Nirmiti (Hindi)*. Itihas Bodh Parkashan, Allahabad.

Srivastava, S. K. 1986. *History of Economic Thought*. Fourth edn. S. Chand & Company Ltd, New Delhi.
Gandhian Theory of Trusteeship has been taken from this book.

Stroup, Atlee L. 1966. *Marriage and Family - A Developmental Approach*. Appleton-Century-Crofts, New York.

United Nations. 2012. Evolution of Income Inequality: Different Time Perspectives and Dimenstions. *Chap. III of: Trade and Development Report*. United Nations Conference on Trade and Development, Geneva.

United Nations. 2015a. *The Millennium Development Goals Report*.

United Nations. 2015b (October). *Transforming our world: the 2030 Agenda for Sustainable Development*.
General Assembly Seventieth session, Agenda items 15 and 116.

Wikipedia. 2016. *Wikipedia, the free encyclopedia*. https://en.wikipedia.org/.
Historical aspects of occupations have partly been taken from Wikipedia. Description of fishing and mining occupations have been taken from this website.

World Bank. 2015. *World Development Indicators*. http://data.worldbank.org/products/wdi.

Index